I0213945

Women Inspired: Volume 4

www.womeninspired.com.au

© Jaya McIntyre and Roxanne McCarty-O'Kane 2025

The creators wish to acknowledge some stories featured in this book shares women's experiences with mental health, domestic violence, sexual abuse and eating disorders. Please read with care. If you are triggered by any content, please seek professional support through a service such as Lifeline 13 11 14, White Ribbon Australia 1800 737 732, or endED 0407 592 932.

This book is sold with the understanding that the featured women are not offering specific personal advice to the reader. For professional or medical advice, seek the services of a suitable, qualified practitioner. The author disclaims any responsibility for liability, loss or risk, personal or otherwise, that happens as a consequence of the use and application of any of the contents of this book.

All rights reserved. This book may not be reproduced in whole or part, stored, posted on the internet, or transmitted in any form or by any means, electronic, mechanical, photocopying, recording, or other, without permission from the author of this book.

Photography by Jaya McIntyre of Empire Art Photography www.empireartphotography.com.au
Stories by Roxanne McCarty-O'Kane www.roxannewriter.com.au
Editing by Melinda Uys www.melindauys.com

Printed by Clark & Mackay www.clark-mackay.com.au

ISBN: 978-0-6450957-5-3 (hardcover)
         978-0-6450957-6-0 (ebook)

NATIONAL LIBRARY OF AUSTRALIA

A catalogue record for this book is available from the National Library of Australia

WOMEN INSPIRED

Volume 4

CONTENTS

Can we sit together, woman to woman, and speak honestly about the beauty we forget to see? We live in an age where storytelling has been overtaken by scripting. Where faces are filtered, bodies reshaped and expressions smoothed until nothing real remains. Where beauty is no longer about presence or personality, but pixel-perfect symmetry. We've traded our wrinkles for retouching, our stories for stills and our uniqueness for conformity.

But what if true beauty was in the story beneath the skin?

There is magic in our lines. They are etched by late nights, deep grief, loud laughter and years of pushing through challenges. There is power in the stretch marks that sing of creation, the freckles that speak of sun-drenched days and the scars that remind us we survived. These are not flaws; they are footnotes in our lived experience.

Still, every scroll delivers a silent message: You should look different. Speak less. Fit in. We are raising a generation not just on impossible beauty standards, but on artificial narratives. Stories manufactured by AI, voices softened to please, faces adjusted to fit the mould. Appearance has become performance. Storytelling has become marketing.

AUTHENTICITY IS NOT OUTDATED. IT'S VITAL. IT'S REVOLUTIONARY.

The world needs your real voice. It needs your face, exactly as it is. We need the unfiltered truth of who you are and where you've been. It's about being seen. It's about self-worth, mental health and reclaiming identity in a world that's trying to edit it out of existence.

When we replace truth with filters, we lose our ability to connect. But when we show up exactly as we are, we give permission for others to do the same. That is the power of real storytelling. That is the power of real women. This is the movement behind Women Inspired.

So, let's choose presence over perfection. Let's tell the raw stories. Let's wear our wrinkles like wisdom and our scars like strength. Let's raise our daughters in a world where being authentic is more beautiful than being airbrushed. Let's be the women who say, "This is what genuine looks like, and it's extraordinary."

Photo by Empire Art Photography of Aimee Sherriff, a reminder that softness and strength can dance together beautifully.

DR. BERNI MORRIS-SMITH

PHARMACIST, PHD MICROBIOLOGIST, RESEARCHER, CLINICAL TRIALS, TELEHEALTH, AUTHOR

When Berni Morris-Smith was five, the large Victorian style hospital wards in England were off limits to young visitors. So, when her mother was diagnosed with breast cancer, Berni and her brother spent many months over a period of two years separated from the one person they needed the most.

Her mum battled behind closed doors in convalescence — if she wasn't in hospital with her dad holding the fort — while Berni counted down the days till they could be together again. It taught her valuable lessons in resilience, courage and faith, things she would need decades later. The consequences of early radiotherapy and lack of cancer-specific drugs meant her mum was sick for many years after surgery. As a young teen, Berni would fetch her mother medicines, carry the shopping and offer comfort in small, quiet ways. It made her feel useful. It made her feel strong.

That quiet drive to care turned into a lifelong career in health and medical research. Berni considered becoming a doctor, but decided on pharmacy at the University of London when she was 16 because she did not want to study for "too many years". Ironically, when Berni embarked on a PhD in microbiology and genetics, she studied longer than a medical doctor! Two years into her thesis, Berni unexpectedly experienced her own health crisis, struck down by a severe post-viral illness now labelled ME (myalgic encephalitis) or chronic fatigue. Officially registered disabled and bed-bound for two years, Berni attributes her recovery to her faith, relentless reading and the love and care of those around her.

Within 12 months of returning to the lab, Berni completed her doctorate in 1991 and opened doors to pioneer the understanding of cellular genetics of bacteria, which was the beginning of the concepts for new cancer medicines. This powerful combination of grace and grit has carried Berni through a remarkable, decades-long career. From conferences in Berlin to presenting research in Los Angeles, Berni has helped shepherd medicines and devices onto markets across Europe, USA, Asia, Latin America and Australia.

After marrying the love of her life, Tim, Australia became home in 1999. Sydney first, where they welcomed two sons, then the Sunshine Coast in 2014, where Berni joined a 200-strong crew commissioning the region's new tertiary hospital. When her husband passed suddenly from stage 4 cancer in 2019, she became an ambassador for the Indigenous non-profit Walk a While in his honour. Tim was key in establishing the elders' self-determined business vision and she visited Haast's Bluff many times with her sons. This deepened her commitment to health equity as the challenges she's witnessed in Central Australia "cannot be unseen."

When Covid-19 hit, Berni stepped onto the frontline in Queensland vaccination hubs while finishing a Graduate Certificate in Aboriginal Studies. That role led to a statewide research post and eventually to co-founding the telehealth model now embedded in the Australian Teletrial Program, bringing cutting-edge studies to rural and remote patients.

With an ever-present humbleness and quiet power, Berni continues to dream up new ways to merge adventure with medicine. With every project Berni considers, she circles back to that original vow: use science, compassion and teamwork to improve patient care.

'WHEN WE HAVE FULFILLMENT, WE HAVE THE COURAGE TO STEP INTO OUR DREAMS.'

— BERNI MORRIS-SMITH

My world fell apart at 4pm on October 16, 2018. One minute my husband Tim and I were on the most magical world trip with our two sons and the next, an oncologist was outlining an aggressive cancer with months – not years – on the clock. It felt as though someone had yanked the floor from under me and handed me a Griefcase too heavy to lift.

Tim and I had always shared big, audacious dreams. He was my best friend, my confidante and the most amazing husband and father. I couldn't bear to contemplate a life without him. With each passing day of hope for a clinical trial or some relief from surgeries, I had to be strong for Tim and our boys while silently adding to the contents of the seemingly infinite Griefcase.

While I tried to capture this experience in my memoir *The Griefcase,* words can never really explain the feeling of losing someone. The first year after Tim's funeral was a blur of paperwork and endless questions of *what if?* that challenged my previously unwavering faith, all while my teenage sons tried to look brave as their hearts splintered. I kept moving with work and attempted to reestablish myself with new friends whilst making sure my boys were okay - anything to drown out the silence at night and alleviate the weight of grief on my chest.

Prior to cancer gripping his body, Tim had been captivated by the vision of a small indigenous community in central Australia. They wanted to place a giant, solar-lit cross on the summit of Memory Mountain as a beacon of hope, tourism and local employment for the Ikuntji people, at Haast's Bluff in Northern Territory. He worked tirelessly to secure vital permits with his renowned business expertise.

When Tim died four months after diagnosis, that cross became my compass. I promised him I would help see it rise, and I ventured out to Memory Mountain several times. It was the place where I felt most connected to Tim and the presence of God. I would speak to both of them while overlooking the sparse Outback landscape stretching to the horizon. When a wedge-tailed eagle - my lifelong symbol of vision and fierce hope - circled overhead during one visit to the mountain, I wept. Not from sadness, but from a strange, holy release.

Grief was still beside me, but on that summit, it shifted from anchor to fuel. My Griefcase transformed into an adventurer's backpack as I made new memories with close friends and my boys. It became a hydration pack as I ran a half-marathon to raise money for Walk a While, something I never thought I could physically achieve. It has morphed into a suitcase as I travel far and wide, including appearing on the Adventure All Stars TV show on a mission to spread even more awareness of Memory Mountain.

The chapters of my life with Tim will always be in my heart and soul. There was an incredible sense of accomplishment when the 22-metre cross finally blazed to life at an Easter ceremony in 2023. Elders sang in language, my eldest son hugged me tight (my youngest was on his first international adventure) and for the first time in years, I felt weightless as we celebrated the legacy Tim left for the Ikuntji people. *We did it, my love!*

Loss hasn't made me fearless, just given me a willingness to be open. To truly listen to my heart and follow what feels fun and adventurous while still fuelled by purpose and supported by those close to me. I love to speak from the heart to encourage others to understand their journey. I still camp under the desert stars, change tires on lonely tracks, drive across rugged outback tracks, present at conferences, empower other women, provide medication reviews and consult on drug trials that might save someone else's Tim. The Griefcase travels with me, but these days it's full of purpose and the quiet certainty that love, once ignited, can ward off any darkness.

WWW.BERNIMORRISSMITH.COM

CHRIS 'CC' CHILDS

FOUNDER OF SAGE LIFE COACHING, ACADEMY OF RESULTS, MY BIG MONEY GOAL, MASTER PRACTITIONER AND TRAINER OF NLP, TIME LINE THERAPY, HYPNOTHERAPY

Chris 'CC' Childs is the kind of person whose energy fills a room and whose wisdom expands across a lifetime. With more than 30 years of experience in business, personal development and property, CC is a powerhouse coach, mentor and Master NLP practitioner and NLP trainer who has built a career on helping others break through what holds them back and step into who they were always meant to be.

Raised on a cattle property in the tiny central Queensland town of Dingo, CC's early years were anything but typical. At the tender age of 10, she was taught to fly a plane, drive a bulldozer and ride a motorbike by her father. That pioneering spirit and sense of adventure, as well as the knowledge she was capable of anything, stayed with her and became the foundation for a life filled with reinvention, resilience and an unshakable belief in human potential.

From the 1980s, she and her husband immersed themselves in self-development, attending seminars, reading every personal growth book they could find and learning from the greats like Tony Robbins, Zig Ziglar and Napoleon Hill. The habits of positivity, grit and continual learning became second nature.

The journey hasn't been without its challenges though. In the aftermath of the GFC and ongoing business pressures, CC experienced profound personal loss. Her 28-year-old son tragically died by suicide in 2011 and in 2022 she suddenly and unexpectedly lost her husband Jack after 43 years of marriage.

Suffering adrenal exhaustion, CC retired and focused on healing and restoring her emotional and physical wellbeing. She reemerged 18 months later with renewed purpose, and created Sage Life Coaching with the desire to combine her decades of coaching clients through wealth, money and mindset with the deep inner work of NLP and Time Line Therapy.

Through personal and business coaching, retreats and Success Summits, CC helps people shift the limiting beliefs and emotional baggage that keep them stuck whether in business, or their personal lives. What sets CC apart isn't just her training, it's her heart. She listens deeply, sees clearly and walks beside her clients as both mentor and cheerleader.

"Real transformation doesn't take months," she says. "With NLP and Time Line Therapy, I see breakthroughs in hours. It gives me goosebumps every time I see the shift, the spark, the realisation of their own power because in that moment, I know they'll never be the same – and neither will I."

From breakthroughs to life-altering mindset shifts, CC brings something rare: equal parts business savvy, personal grit and genuine care. CC goes far beyond surface-level motivation; she helps people rewire the patterns that quietly shape their lives.

"Everyone you admire has had a coach or mentor," she says. "The question isn't whether coaching works, it's whether you're ready to let someone help you reach the next level." With CC, the breakthrough you've been waiting for might be closer than you think.

'WHEN YOU CHANGE THE WAY YOU LOOK AT THINGS, THE THINGS YOU LOOK AT CHANGE.'
– WAYNE DYER

Standing in front of 250 people in the Maroochydore RSL function room in 2014, I looked around the room. My clients were all sitting at round tables with white tablecloths and centrepieces that reflected the same colour scheme as the red, black and silver balloon fountains.

I was there to teach the concepts I admired from Jane Atwood's book The Passion Test and asked the audience to indulge me as I read out the two-page description of my business. As I made it through the content, which included descriptions of red folders of information, amazing websites and online programs, a bold vision for the reach and what I was going to teach, I moved to the description of what was going on in that very room that day… "and I'm standing in front of 250 people in a huge room with round tables, white table cloths, centrepieces and red black and silver balloon fountains."

As people were wondering what the point of all of this was, I stated, "I wrote this in 2011 after my son took his life and I was struggling to know whether I would move forward with my business or not." At the time, my branding was orange and there was no sign of the folders bursting with course content and knowledge I had accumulated over the years, no amazing website and a very limited number of clients.

These results and my success had all come about because it was my passion. I had set my goals with a burning desire and total belief that allowed my unconscious mind and my RAS - Reticular Activating System – to work together to give me exactly what I'd asked for. My results were tangible, and I received a standing ovation.

This success came from The Passion Test, a goal setting process I still teach today. I combine goal setting, value alignment, and the skills I have gained through NLP and Time Line Therapy to assist my clients in achieving their goals easily and effortlessly.

Before I retired, many saw me as a successful, confident and powerful businesswoman. What they didn't see were the debilitating self-limiting beliefs that held me back. I struggled deeply with my sense of self-worth and the value of my contribution, despite decades of experience behind me. It wasn't until 2024 when I discovered NLP, Time Line Therapy and hypnotherapy that everything shifted. I was able to shed those false self-assumptions and align my values with my goals. From that moment, I began achieving with ease and clarity. My life transformed. I felt reborn. Empowered. Bulletproof. That's the experience I now live for, helping others feel that same unshakable strength and freedom within themselves.

I came out of retirement because I knew I wasn't finished; there was more I wanted to do. I realised changing people's lives is one my highest values. I no longer hide from the impact I've made; I own it with purpose. I'm here to help people unlock their inner strength, break free from limiting beliefs, and build unshakable confidence.

Whether it's in business, weight loss, or stepping out from the shadows of self-doubt, I guide others from lived experience, not theory. My mission is to help people align their goals with their values so they can create the life they've only dreamed of, easily and effortlessly. This is more than coaching: it's a movement. Because when one person transforms, the ripple reaches far beyond. And I'm here to change the world, one powerful person at a time.

WWW.SAGELIFECOACHING.COM.AU

CLAIRE SMITH

MANAGING DIRECTOR OF FORBES MEISNER PTY LTD, AUTHOR, SPEAKER, AUSTRALIAN OF THE YEAR, LOCAL HERO FOR QUEENSLAND 2025

When people tell Claire Smith, "You can't do that," she simply flashes one of her dazzling smiles and proves them wrong. Power, passion and determination well up from within her: nothing stands in this woman's way.

A fierce advocate for creativity, innovation and compassion, Claire has carved out a life that defies limits. Her unwavering self-belief paired with a boundless curiosity has taken her across industries, causes and communities with one mission in mind: to create meaningful change and lift others as she goes.

As the founder of Wildlife Rescue Sunshine Coast, Claire built Queensland's first volunteer-run, 24/7 wildlife rescue service from the ground up. What began as a shared dream with three friends has grown into a life-saving force that educates, rescues and rehabilitates, offering not just care to native animals, but hope to a nation increasingly aware of its environmental responsibilities.

It was this tireless work that saw Claire honoured as the Australian of the Year - Local Hero for Queensland in 2025. But she doesn't just speak for animals; Claire speaks for *anyone* who doesn't have a voice. As an active member of Owls for Justice, she is a powerful ally for child protection and justice, using her influence to advocate at all levels of government and society.

These are just a few threads that make up Claire's rich life tapestry. She's been a diesel mechanic at Alltype Diesel, led sustainable projects, managed Research and Development (R&D) at Hahn Environmental and brought innovation to the forefront of engineering operations.

Her technical savvy transitioned seamlessly into her work as Managing Director of Forbes Meisner Pty Ltd, specialising in R&D Tax Incentives. And as Business Advisor in Residence at the Innovation Centre Sunshine Coast, she mentored countless entrepreneurs and startups, guiding bold ideas from spark to reality.

Claire's creative spark is as fierce as her professional drive. She's been a singer in an all-female rock band performing to tens of thousands of fans on tour, an actor on stage, TV and film and the owner and editor-in-chief of four community newspapers. She's written and illustrated children's books, penned scripts and inspired audiences as a sought-after keynote speaker and mentor. Whether she's speaking about innovation, courage or compassion, Claire's message is always clear "Believe in yourself, and don't wait for permission to lead".

Ask her what she's most proud of, and she'll tell you without hesitation: being Mum to two amazing sons and Grandma Claire to two beautiful granddaughters. Right behind that? Raising over $600,000 to help wildlife carers after the devastating 2019 bushfires, establishing Queensland's first kangaroo hospital, securing two ambulances for injured animals and inspiring everyday people to step up, speak out and make a difference.

Claire Smith is living proof that you don't have to fit into one box - or any box at all. She's a trailblazer, protector, creator and coach. But above all, she's a believer. In people. In possibility. In the quiet but unstoppable power of self-belief.

Claire Smith is living proof that you don't have to fit into one box - or any box at all. She's a trailblazer, protector, creator and coach. But above all, she's a believer. In people. In possibility. In the quiet but unstoppable power of self-belief.

THE ONLY WAY TO ACHIEVE THE IMPOSSIBLE IS TO BELIEVE IT IS POSSIBLE

– CHARLES KINGSLEIGH

O ver 40 years ago, I stood in a 30,000-strong human barrier around the nine-mile perimeter fence of a US air base housing nuclear missiles. It was at the Greenham Common Women's Peace Camp in England, and it's a memory that will always ignite a spark of strength in me.

What struck me about Greenham wasn't just the scale of the protest, but the spirit of love behind it. There was no fear, even when we knew we'd be physically removed by police or had our belongings bulldozed. We were standing against something enormous, yet it never felt hopeless.

In the 1980s, I'd go to the Women's Peace Camp for months at a time, drawn in by the energy, the purpose and the fierce commitment to peaceful resistance. There were a number of camps located around the air base, but the Green Gate, where I often stayed, was known for its wild spirit. That's where I really woke up to the women's movement and the raw, undeniable power of collective female action.

At Greenham, grandmothers, mothers and kids all stood side by side, linked by the shared belief that we could change the world if we truly believed in what we were doing. That experience shaped me because it wasn't just about politics or peace; it was about knowing, deep in your bones, the power of women who stood their ground.

That legacy of women's strength, resilience and solidarity lives on in me, and I carry it everywhere I go; it was a spark waiting to be set alight from the moment I was born. The midwife had looked at me and told my mother, "This one's been here before." My parents armed me with solid beliefs and values that have remained the foundation of all that I do and have never let me down; you can be anything you want to be; always eat good food; always buy good shoes; learn to play a musical instrument; always be polite; be kind; never be greedy.

With my parents' support, I never questioned my place in my world. I just knew I was here to be me and to achieve whatever I set my mind to. It wasn't until I was at high school that I saw a huge disparity between how I'd been brought up and the social norm. It was incredibly challenging to understand the constraints being instilled on us in the classroom - I was having none of that nonsense.

I left school with bugger all qualifications, but my unwavering self-belief has allowed me to do everything I wanted, when I've wanted to do it. *That* is the measure of my success: live life for today, not for next week, next month or somewhere in the future.

After the thrill of seeing my face on a flag waving in Canberra at the Australian of the Year Awards, I'm taking my keynote presentations, which centre around curiosity and creativity, on the road. I've spent years in front of cameras and crowds; I'm never shy to speak up! But while a lot of what I share, especially about wildlife and conservation, is serious and important, I've always believed in the power of humour to connect and make messages stick.

My comedic sensibilities began in primary school, where I was so tiny my uniform was custom made. I stood out, and not in a good way. I learned quickly that if I made people laugh, they wouldn't pick on me. That skill of using humour to disarm and engage has stayed with me ever since and now it's central to how I inspire, inform and challenge audiences today. I might just be one small spark, but it only takes one to ignite a fire that lights the dark and warms the cold, that makes change possible and a better world a reality.

FRANCHESCA BLANDON

FOUNDER OF MEDUSA ALLURE BEAUTY STUDIO, HAIR AND MAKEUP DIRECTOR AUSTRALIAN WEARABLE ART FESTIVAL

Born in Costa Rica, Fran moved permanently with her children to the Sunshine Coast, Queensland, in late 2015. It was a courageous move, but when you dig deeper into this powerful woman's story, you quickly realise the enormous strength, energy and tenacity encased within her small frame. A career spanning more than 17 years in the beauty industry, with an impressive reputation as a qualified hairdresser, professional stylist and makeup artist, is just the start.

Fran wields a creative reach which goes far beyond traditional beauty. She is also a highly skilled and passionate visual artist, known for her work in full body paint, special effects, airbrushing, ultraviolet (black light) art, headpiece and costume design, canvas and wall art, creative photography and digital art. Her ability to blend these disciplines into stunning visual storytelling sets her apart as a true creative force.

This long list of knowledge and skill substantiates the sense that there is no 'dabbling' in Fran's world: just focus, accomplishment and expertise. She is certified in advanced cosmetic tattooing, including ombre brows, feather touch, eyeliner and nano lips, as well as skin needling and BB glow therapies.

She is the founder of Medusa Allure Beauty Studio in Sippy Downs, a space created to combine all her specialties under one roof. Here, clients are treated to a highly personalised and professional experience, where Fran uses only high-end, FDA-approved products and HD cosmetics to deliver exceptional results. Her attention to detail and artistic eye ensures each client walks away feeling confident and completely transformed.

Running a business, creating art and caring for clients and her three sons is hectic on the best of days, but Fran has still more energy for other worthy roles, with the most high-profile being her position as Hair and Makeup Director for the Australian Wearable Art Festival. In this role, she personally recruits and leads a team of around 25 emerging and experienced hair and makeup artists across four major shows. The event features over 40 national and international artists and models and Fran plays a key part in bringing the bold, avant-garde looks to life on stage. Her leadership, creativity and professionalism have become a hallmark of the festival's success.

Throughout her career, Fran has been recognised with numerous awards for her artistry. At the Australian Body Art Festival, she earned multiple first-place and people's choice awards in categories such as Special Effects, Airbrush and UV Full Body Art. She has also taken out top honours at the Brisbane Hair and Beauty Expo in various professional artist divisions. In 2024, she was invited to serve as an official judge at the Australian Body Art Awards, a reflection of her industry expertise and influence.

Whether painting bodies, designing costumes, directing creative teams, or offering personalised beauty services, Fran's dedication, vision and boundless creativity are an inspiration. Akin to the Medusa that has been linked to her since she was a teenager, Fran is the epitome of feminine strength, beautiful courage and powerful determination.

'KEEP YOUR EYES ON THE STARS, AND YOUR FEET ON THE GROUND.'
– THEODORE ROOSEVELT

Medusa was a nickname thrust upon me by my high school peers because I had crazy hair I struggled to tame. When the time came to create my own business decades later, the Medusa was a clear image in my mind.

Once misunderstood and even demonised, Medusa has been reclaimed as a figure who represents women owning their power, beauty and voice. Her iconic image is striking, bold and visually captivating. This aligns perfectly with my creative style and my studio's offerings because it's not about blending in - it's about being authentic and unapologetically yourself, embracing your own kind of beauty.

I discovered a passion for hair and makeup while experimenting with spooky looks over many Halloweens while growing up in a middle-class family in Costa Rica. I thrived in the freedom of teaching myself different techniques to achieve looks I found fascinating…then using myself and my cousins as guinea pigs.

When my family planned to move to my stepfather's homeland, the United States, I made the bold decision to stay in Costa Rica. I was just 17 years old. It was a turning point, and I had to grow up fast. I finished high school, lived in my aunt's house and juggled full-time work with night classes. I even joined a cheerleading team and trained several nights a week. Life was full, fast-paced and challenging, but I thrived on the independence.

In my first marriage, we were together for nearly ten years and had a son but eventually went our separate ways. Later, I met my second husband at work. We had two more beautiful boys, and I started my career as a qualified hair and makeup artist before we moved to Australia in 2015, seeking a better life. While our intention was to create more balance, a lack of communication and a change in my husband's job role to include frequent travel slowly created a disconnect between us.

Meanwhile, our arrival in Australia led me to follow creative pursuits and I discovered a true passion for body art. A producer of the Australian Body Art Festival (ABAF) encouraged me to enter after seeing the UV light fantasy makeup creations I was sharing on Instagram.

I entered several competitions between 2015 and 2021 and loved the challenge. Because I wasn't bound by conventional rules taught in the classroom, I could think outside the box with my art. My entry in special effects category at the 2017 ABAF was a gargoyle complete with custom-made horns. The uniqueness shocked the judges, but I received the people's choice award that year, which was much more satisfying.

After several attempts to repair my marriage, we parted ways for good in early 2021. But in October 2022, while we were in the legal process to finalise our divorce, he took his own life. While dealing with our grief from his sudden loss, I was thrust into a legal fight that lasted 18 months to reclaim my rights after his death.

I was forced to dig deep to find the strength for my family and redirect my energy to my boys, whose stability and wellbeing was my number one priority. I've gained a stronger sense of self and deep appreciation for my own resilience throughout that process.

Now, I've stepped unapologetically into my Medusa era - I am bold, brave, creative and unique. I surround myself with people who lift me up and provide me with unconditional support, and I'm ready to help women from all walks of life unlock their inner beauty.

WWW.MEDUSAALLURE.COM.AU

JENNY LAWSON

FOUNDER AND DIRECTOR OF SUCCESSFUL GRANTS, SUNSHINE COAST BUSINESS WOMEN'S NETWORK OUTSTANDING BUSINESS WOMAN OF THE YEAR 2024

Jenny Lawson is a visionary who turns bold questions into transformative action. From creating and managing three high-performing physiotherapy clinics, to building the nationally respected consultancy, Successful Grants, Jenny has led with heart, intelligence and a fearless drive to create meaningful change.

Courageous and eye-wateringly energetic, this thrill-seeker never set out to be a grant writer. For three decades, she was a respected physiotherapist with specialisations in paediatrics, sport and disability. She served on national boards, managed clinics and mentored young clinicians. But in 2008, while volunteering at the Mooloolaba Outrigger Club, where she also paddled competitively, Jenny decided to try her hand at writing a grant submission.

She knew it had the potential to be a more efficient way to fundraise than flipping sausages at weekend barbecues. It was. Within two years, Jenny had helped the club secure $1.1 million for infrastructure, equipment and safety upgrades. Word spread. Requests grew. Jenny soon found herself at a crossroads: continue in physiotherapy, or step into something entirely new.

It was a brave decision to walk away from a well-established career and businesses to pursue a path unknown, but Jenny has always had an adventurous and competitive spirit and this served her well. Her ability to listen, interpret complex needs and translate them into compelling grant submissions that tick every box and tell a powerful story has seen Successful Grants evolve into an award-winning consultancy with local heart and national reach.

Now, she leads a highly skilled team of writers who support over 150 organisations a year, securing upwards of $10 million in grant funding, which fuel everything from grassroots sports to advanced manufacturing, health initiatives and arts festivals. But behind the impressive dollar figures is a deeper drive: to help others shine by equipping them with tools to grow, survive and be recognised.

Jenny's approach sets her apart. She brings the ethics and professionalism of healthcare into the often-unregulated world of grant writing. She's transparent, pragmatic and deeply invested in her clients' success. If a project isn't aligned or lacks a competitive edge, she'll say so… then offer alternative strategies to achieve the outcome in a better way.

Jenny has built a sustainable, flexible business model that empowers her team to grow in their own strengths. She works from home, builds in time for family and community and continues to invest in mentoring others. In 2024, Jenny was recognised as the Outstanding Business Woman of the Year by the Sunshine Coast Business Women's Network, a fitting tribute to the strength, clarity and leadership she brings to every facet of her life.

Looking ahead, Jenny sees Successful Grants evolving again. She's preparing to take on more board roles and philanthropic advisory work, while handing the reins of day-to-day operations to full-time team members. Her goal remains clear: to keep helping people realise their potential through funding, recognition, and the confidence to take their own bold steps.

'YOU LEARN FROM EVERY EXPERIENCE YOU ARE BRAVE ENOUGH TO PUT YOUR HAND UP FOR.'

– JENNY LAWSON

Adventure has been my greatest teacher. I've travelled across continents with nothing but a backpack and a curious mind, been charged by a lioness in Zimbabwe, climbed trees to avoid elephants, hiked Hinchinbrook Island carrying everything I needed on my back and paddled outrigger canoes across oceans. Each experience has taught me something about resilience, resourcefulness and how little we truly need to find joy.

My first big adventure was South America at 21, where I learned to trust my instincts and stretch every dollar. We had to wrap our backpacks in chicken wire to stop them being slashed; I learned very quickly what it meant to be privileged and what it meant to respect other people's space and stories. Next came Africa, which featured six months of rough roads, close calls with wildlife and moments of breathtaking wonder that taught me how to think on my feet and how deeply connected we all are, no matter our culture or language.

While I'd grown up with a surf ski paddling on the Brisbane River, outrigging came into my life while working in Townsville in the '90s. It was new, physical and required early morning commitment. I loved it instantly. Today, it keeps me grounded. There's something magical about gliding through water in the dark, watching the sun rise over the ocean with a team of strong women beside me. We train hard, compete fiercely and laugh often. It keeps me humble and stokes the competitive fire that keeps me pushing in all areas of life.

While we've had incredible victories on the water, I've tasted defeat too. I trained for six months to make the Masters team to represent Australia in Rio and missed out by one spot. That one stung, but it taught me that the effort, the grit and the community matter more than the medal.

Adventure is also in the everyday. I've hiked with my husband and three children, showing them how to carry their gear, light fires and respect nature's rhythms. We've done five-day hikes with dehydrated food, freezing nights and shared stories around the campfire. Those are the moments that shape a family and memories I treasure dearly.

One of the most meaningful hikes was back to Hinchinbrook Island, a place I took boyfriends to test their mettle. It's where I got engaged to the love of my life—who passed the test! —and later took our children to show them how capable they are. They don't remember the tantrums or the blisters, just the adventure. That's a win for me.

I've paddled 37km around Magnetic Island, jumping in and out of a moving canoe mid-race. I've competed in Hawaii with a team of women driven by strength, strategy and sisterhood. I've learned that most challenges, whether physical or emotional, feel less daunting when you've built your courage muscle by doing hard things on purpose.

Adventure has also shaped the way I see risk. When you've hitchhiked through South Africa (sorry Mum), pushed a broken-down van past wild animals, or paddled into unpredictable ocean swells, you stop fearing the unknown so much. You learn to assess, trust your team then back yourself. That mindset has carried through to every part of my life. I've made bold decisions, leaving careers, starting new ventures, putting my name to things that might not work out. But I've never let fear be the reason I didn't try.

Travel taught me that the most meaningful growth often sits just past the edge of your comfort zone. For me, adventure isn't a break from life. It's how I live it. These are the ingredients that make my life incredible and traits I encourage everyone to embrace in their own worlds.

KALLY MARSHALL

OWNER SENSORY SUPER HEROES, FOUNDER OF SAFE TO BEE MENTORING, EMPATHETIC STORYLISTENER, RESTORATIVE STORYTELLER, SENSORY STRATEGIST

Radiating joy, bouncing with energy, and lighting up the room, Kally Marshall has always moved through the world a little differently. But it was one heck of a story that led her to harness her neurodivergence as a strength, one she could use to *tune in* to those with spicy brains and big feelings. As with any superhero origin story, the first chapter centred around discovering her own hidden talents.

Kally spent her professional life working behind the scenes on high-pressure government projects. As big-picture thinking came naturally to her, she had a knack for making sense of tangled systems and an intuitive empathy that helped her understand individual and group dynamics with ease. But while she thrived in collaborative projects and creative problem-solving, everyday tasks like remembering appointments or finishing paperwork often slipped through the cracks. It was a contrast that confused even her: how could someone so capable in chaos forget the simplest of things?

Ever the glass-half-full thinker, Kally spent much of her adult life giving herself pep talks and signing up for personal development courses to try to improve the areas where she struggled. When Kally focused on one area, it improved, only for another to slip. Well-meaning advice followed, which she eagerly applied. To outsiders, her 'misses' seemed like normal busyness or forgetfulness, and Kally was reassured that it was typical to drop the ball sometimes. But it was exhausting, and some days it became impossible to function.

It wasn't until she sat down with a psychologist, heart open, that the pieces finally began to fall into place. The answer: ADHD and Autism. "It explained everything; how I felt, how I worked, why I'd completely forget some things and obsess over others. I'd always felt like I was too much… too talkative, too messy, too loud, too slow, too disorganised, too late, too enthusiastic, too generous…," Kally shares.

The more she unsuccessfully tried to fix those traits, the more shame she carried for simply being herself. She began to shrink and fear that she was somehow fundamentally faulty. Some professionals call this 'masking,' a term Kally initially didn't relate to because she was so innately open! In time, she understood that masking is an unconscious behaviour, one she had learned over her lifetime.

Eventually, Kally came to recognise she was beautifully wired for something different. She co-founded Sensory Super Heroes, a business creating tools to support regulation and wellbeing, with her sister Jenna. Their lap blankets, calming swings and handmade crash bags are used in homes, schools, and clinics across Australia.

Kally now deeply understands the brain-body connection, and how to create the internal safety that allows people to thrive. Her knowledge of the eight sensory systems, paired with genuine curiosity and care, helps children and caregivers alike to feel Safe to Bee themselves through her unique mentoring program. Kally's journey has taught her that gold is often found in small, quiet moments shared with like-minded people who are also on the journey. A shift in language. A giggle after tears. A question you weren't sure you were allowed to ask. Because when the nervous system feels safe, everything else becomes possible.

'TUNE IN. JOIN IN.'

– KALLY MARSHALL

I'm getting good at being a terrible parent. I've been practicing it for 10 years. It sounds shocking, but guess what? Being good at being a terrible parent is also what makes me a *great* parent. As a neurodivergent mother, I forget things. I'm often late. I have a habit of forgetting to order tuckshop for my girls. But as I have come to better understand these things about myself, and I communicate them openly to my husband and our children, I can demonstrate that life is about learning from your mistakes, not being ashamed of them.

Here's a case in point: my daughter had been on a waitlist for gymnastics for *ages* and was over the moon when she got the call to say she was in. We made it the first Thursday and she loved it. However, I got a call from after school care the following Thursday: my daughter had remembered, I had forgotten. My heart hurt deeply that day. It was new to our routine, and I hadn't yet integrated it into my mind and family rhythm.

My seven-year-old daughter didn't get mad. She didn't shame me. She didn't try to give me advice or tell me I should try harder. When I cried she reassured me and said, "That's okay, Mum. It worked out well, they cooked my favourite food at after-school care. It was delicious! We can just go next week."

The following Thursday morning, she handed me a colourful, practical reminder – a pink note that read 'It's gymnastics day.' Because she knew that I was highly likely to lose it, she paused and then deliberately pinned it to my chest. I gave her the biggest, squeeziest hug and wore it all day. To Pilates, to work and the shops. Guess what? We made it. Our kids have so much to teach us about how to be loving, creative, courageous, and kind. I am so grateful that I am learning from the best!

Up until the age of 38, I felt like I was failing at something everyone else had mastered. I internalised every missed deadline, every burnt meal, every flippant comment that I was too much, as proof that I was faulty. Even well-meaning advice chipped away at my self-worth because I told myself I had to cover up my differences and do better.

When 'doing better' wasn't working, I found the words to communicate what I found difficult and why. This created an opportunity for everyone to meet me where I was at in those areas and allowed me to fully embrace my strengths again. It takes bravery to be so open with the people around us, but believe me, it's worth it.

This works both ways. When it comes to discovering sensory strategies for neurodivergent families, one of my favourite philosophies is, "Join In." If a child is doing something like hanging upside down off the couch, they are naturally self-regulating. That movement stimulates the vestibular system, located in the inner ear, which helps with balance, coordination, and body awareness. The best thing you can do is join them. Lie next to them. Notice how good it feels. You don't have to talk about it (in fact, I would really encourage you not to), just be there.

That simple act says, "I see you, I trust you and I could learn something from you." Take it from me; joining in can be a lot harder than it sounds. It can feel wildly uncomfortable for adults, especially when the behaviour looks unusual, loud, messy, or inappropriate by typical standards. Things like repeating made-up sounds, smelling food before eating, lying face down on the grass or crashing onto the couch might not look like regulation, but it is. Challenge yourself not to apply that 'auto-correct' parenting voice and instead, pause, stay curious, and (when it's safe to do so) join in. That's where connections grow.

I love listening to people's stories. I seem to naturally spark light, meaningful conversations that gently shift the heavy stuff aside. This helps people reconnect with their own sense of safety, so real, lasting change happens. At the end of the day, we're all just trying to find balance, connection, and safety for our nervous system. When we create space for everyone to feel Safe To Bee who they truly are, the entire world becomes brighter.

WWW.SENSORYSUPERHEROES.COM // WWW.SAFETOBEE.COM.AU

WHAT INSPIRES YOU TO DO WHAT YOU DO?

CLAIRE SMITH

My drive comes from a strong sense of responsibility to stand up for the vulnerable, ensuring their voices are heard and their needs met. This purpose fuels my passion and commitment to make a meaningful difference in the world. As an activator and change-maker, I approach opportunities with a strong belief in my abilities and the mindset that I can achieve anything I set my mind to. This has been a defining trait throughout my life, but I've learned it can sometimes challenge others. Rather than let this hold me back, it has fuelled my passion for empowering others—particularly women—to find their voice, own their power and embrace their potential to create change.

KALLY MARSHALL

What drives me is the phenomenal number of broken adults who've crossed my path in recent years. Each one has shared a story that's both heartbreaking and familiar. They have lived their lives misunderstood. They weren't faulty, they were neurodivergent, and no one saw it. No one had the language or support to help them see it themselves, until the damage was done. I've witnessed the pain that comes from generations of undiagnosed neurodivergence, and I'm determined to help change that story. I do this work so that the next generation grows up feeling seen, safe and celebrated for who they are.

LILLIAN MUCHIRI

I am very privileged to be born into an era where I can look back on decades of turmoil and see the potential for a shift. My early experiences did not break me, but they made me brave and insightful, and taught me resilience. When I speak with children in Australia and we compare my experiences and those of others still in my village, the plight of their overseas counterparts touches them, and they would do anything to help. They encourage me to continue to share my stories. I will keep going, with much support from my mum, sisters, community and well-wishers. We will inspire a change, however small: we won't stop.

MEL PAYNE

To inspire myself to keep going, I reflect on how far I've come, the moments I doubted myself or wondered if I was enough; I remind myself that I did the hard things anyway. Those milestones sustain me and give me strength, especially knowing I've built a life and career that once felt out of reach. I surround myself with people who uplift me; my family, mentors and colleagues, and I take time to celebrate the small wins. I'm inspired by staying connected to my 'why', even when it's hard. It's about showing up fully, even on the days when no one's watching.

STACY McCRAY

I'm inspired by curiosity, connection and the joy of life-long learning. I'm especially moved by women who rise after lifequakes, rebuilding with heart and strength. Doing less often creates more; space invites alignment and joy becomes the compass. I'm now guided by a spiritual way of living that prioritises presence, growth and authenticity. My wellbeing is grounded in four core pillars: sleep, movement, nutrition and mindset. Through meditation, music, nature walks, dancing and daily rituals, I raise my vibration and stay aligned with what matters most. These practices support my vitality and energise me through meaningful social connections and community.

YVONNE PURVIS

I do this work because I know what it's like to feel stuck, to crave more, and to wonder if true change is possible. I've lived that reality and I know what happens when you decide to rewrite your story and claim the life you desire. What drives me is the fire inside every woman who's ready to step into her next level, who refuses to settle, and who knows she's meant for more. Because when a woman fully steps into her power, she not only transforms her own life but the world around her.

DR. KAREN SUTHERLAND

CERTIFIED AI CONSULTANT AND SENIOR LECTURER AT THE UNIVERSITY OF THE SUNSHINE COAST, AUTHOR, SPEAKER, DIRECTOR OF DHARANA DIGITAL

Dr. Karen Sutherland isn't your typical academic. Yes, she's a Certified AI Consultant, Senior Lecturer at the University of the Sunshine Coast and multi-award-winning author, but she grew up in a working-class family and was the first in her immediate circle to attend university. Yes, Karen is an expert in the digital space, but she is also wholly committed to a lifestyle rooted in ancient yogic practice. Rather than buck against these fundamental contrasts, she has harnessed them to connect with people both in and outside of academia.

For Karen, her focus is not on collecting status or titles, it's on helping others make sense of the complex, and using communication as a bridge between confusion and clarity. Driven by deep curiosity and a strong desire to demystify what often feels overwhelming, she has carved out a space where the language of AI and social media is translated into something accessible, relatable and actionable.

Karen has worked across a wide range of sectors in public relations and communications, from entertainment and government to corporate and nonprofit: iconic shows like *Neighbours* and *Stingers* and organisations such as ABC TV and the Australian Red Cross Blood Service have all had the benefit of her expertise. These real-world experiences inform everything she does.

Through her business, Dharana Digital, Karen helps wellness-based organisations and others embrace AI tools to safely and ethically increase efficiency and reduce costs. Her hands-on approach is strategic and impactful. Karen believes theory only becomes meaningful when you can show how it works in real life, which is why she continues to keep one foot firmly in the industry while lecturing and researching at UniSC. "You can't only speak vaguely about theoretical concepts," she says. "You have to bring them to life."

It's unsurprising then that Karen's second book, *Strategic Social Media Management – Theory and Practice*, became one of the most downloaded texts of its kind globally. Her fifth book, *Artificial Intelligence for Strategic Communication*, is due to follow suit.

Karen has picked up numerous accolades, including 2023 and 2024 Book Excellence Awards and several international Stevie Awards, including Woman of the Year – Social Media. She's also a regular commentator on global news platforms like The Wall Street Journal, Sky News, Nine News, ABC News, SBS and the international streaming service Ticker.

Despite being an introvert deeply ensconced in the digital world, Karen has built a career centred around human connection. She's a powerful public speaker, a respected consultant and an educator with a gift for guiding others through unfamiliar territory. Since 2007, her daily yoga practice has kept her grounded; it is a quiet constant in an ever-changing digital world.

Ultimately, Karen's purpose is simple: to empower others to consciously embrace technology, not fear it, and to show that no matter where you start, it's possible to make a meaningful impact with authenticity, humility and heart.

'IN THE END, ALL THAT WILL MATTER IS WHO YOU BECAME. AND HOW MANY YOU HELPED.'

– ROBIN SHARMA

'␣ve always lived in the space between two worlds - one ancient, one emerging. On one hand, I've been deeply committed to yoga since 2007 and on the other, I've found myself at the forefront of digital innovation riding the crest of first social media, and now the AI wave.

At first glance, they seem contradictory - how can chanting, meditation and karma yoga possibly co-exist with algorithmic models, machine learning and digital strategy? But for me, they're entirely complementary. Yoga taught me stillness and self-regulation; social media and AI fuel my curiosity and desire to help others navigate complex systems. Both keep me anchored in different ways.

I came to yoga during one of the lowest points in my life: I was feeling so overwhelmed and lost. I Googled "silent retreat" and stumbled across Rocklyn Yoga Ashram, about two hours from where I lived in Melbourne. I booked nine days without knowing what I was walking into.

When I arrived, I immediately wanted to leave. It was far from the Westernised Lululemon yoga of my local gym. The ashram was dedicated to authentic, traditional yoga: chanting, service-based karma yoga, meditation and quiet reflection.

But the longer I stayed, something shifted. I started to feel peace. I'd never experienced stillness like that before. Since then, yoga has been my daily practice. It's the constant that helps me show up in a world that's always in flux.

I travel to India regularly, revisit the same ashram every year and even subscribe to what we call the "digital ashram," which are weekly Zoom sessions with spiritual teachers with decades of experience. A few years ago, I felt ready to teach and began sharing yoga with others. I waited a long time to ensure my own foundation was solid, and I'm glad I did. Yoga isn't something I dip in and out of; it's a way of life.

In contrast, my work in AI emerged from a desire to help people make sense of technology before it overwhelmed them. I saw the potential early and leaned in, first as a learner, then a consultant, and now as a researcher and author.

I became certified in the AI Persona Method developed by Jeff J Hunter in the US, completed studies at the University of Sydney and started experimenting. I love watching people's minds open when they see what AI can do - and then I help them understand what it *shouldn't* do. Bad AI-generated content is everywhere.

When researching for *Artificial intelligence for Strategic Communication*, I interviewed scholars, AI developers, marketers and communicators and surveyed 400 professionals from eight countries across the combined sample. What resulted was a road-map based on real-world insight and practical experience. And, like yoga, it was as much a learning journey for me as it was a resource for others.

I love the juxtaposition of yoga and AI. One ancient, the other advancing faster than we can sometimes keep up with. But both have shaped who I am. Yoga grounds me. AI challenges me. And in that space where silence meets strategy, I've found a unique balance that lets me serve others around the globe.

It all comes back to connection, curiosity and helping people find calm clarity in the chaos.

WWW.DRKARENSUTHERLAND.COM // LINKEDIN: KARENESUTHERLAND

KELLY SMITH

FOUNDER OF FAST PSYCHOLOGY, LAWYER, PROPERTY DEVELOPER, FOUNDER OF URBAN COCOON, CO-FOUNDER OF SAN CHURRO

Belting out a karaoke banger seems about as quiet as it gets for Kelly Smith, a woman who has poured herself into a plethora of high-end careers, faced every role with grit and graft, and point-blank refused to settle for ordinary. She is dynamic, authentic and completely enthralling; every chapter is a lesson in industriousness and self-belief. Yet under that power, energy and experience lies a stillness and peace. To fathom the gamut of trials and tests she has undertaken (and emerged triumphant from) to arrive on the Sunshine Coast is a journey in itself.

Raised in a single-parent household where her mum worked late nights as a chef, Kelly was taught resilience by necessity. Determined to avoid the financial struggle she saw at home, she passed over her preferred area of psychology and launched into law school instead. Armed with her degree and London-bound, it wasn't the destination that would change the trajectory of her life, but reading a statistic in an article on the way. *Men were 20 times more likely to apply for jobs beyond their qualifications.* 35000 ft in the air everything shifted, and a belief cracked open. She didn't need to wait to be 'ready'. She stepped off the plane with a clear motto: "Aim just beyond where you are, and grow into it." It would inform almost every juncture of her life.

Kelly began her career with Price Waterhouse Coopers in London, was poached by a client and co-founded a consulting firm in the Netherlands to combine her legal training with systems thinking; she was the bridge between tech and law. The business thrived, she excelled, but knew inherently that life was passing her by. Kelly worked in beautiful places like Denmark and Ireland, but never actually *saw* them. It was another seismic shift that would shake up her entire world. While visiting her fiancé in New York, they mapped out a year of adventure, Kelly sold her share of the business, and they hit the road. She learned flamenco in Spain, rode camels through the Sahara, dived in the Red Sea and lived next door to a nonna in Rome. In all that beautiful living, a churros-fuelled weekend in Madrid became the inspiration behind Australia's most beloved dessert franchise businesses.

Kelly was pregnant with the first of her two children when she co-founded San Churro, and opened the first store when her son was just two weeks old. With zero franchising experience but a deep belief in the product, she built an empire of more than 50 stores. Aiming 'just beyond' saw her become a finalist in the Telstra Business Women's Awards, earned her multiple accolades and recognition as one of Australia's most prominent female founders alongside the likes of Boost Juice's Janine Allis and Healthy Habits' Katherine Sampson.

In 2022, Kelly returned to study, this time to an area she had always felt innately drawn to: psychology. She launched Fast Psychology in 2023, a no-fluff, results-driven approach to helping people navigate tough decisions, tricky conversations and emotional overwhelm. She has excelled in this new venture against a backdrop of divorce and interstate moves, but then, why wouldn't she? Through every chapter - lawyer, consultant, entrepreneur, psychology guru – the one constant has been her unwavering belief that she would grow into 'it'.

A childhood of scarcity made her alert to risk and hungry for opportunity. Even in the 'quiet' moments of karaoke, Kelly is already thinking, *what's next?* It's her very own superpower.

'EVERYTHING YOU WANT IS JUST OUTSIDE YOUR COMFORT ZONE.'
– ROBERT ALLEN

'm inspired by anyone living slightly off-script. Those who choose silence in a noisy world. The people who do their thing no matter what; the single mum who still shows up; the woman who dares to be seen no matter how messy, powerful or unfinished; the leader who admits they're scared but still steps up.

I've been fortunate to have experienced the traditional style of success. The multi-million-dollar business, the awards, the family with the large home. But I now stand for a very different kind of success. Not the shiny, performative, burnout-inducing kind, but the grounded kind from within.

We've been sold the idea that happiness lives on the other side of achievement. That more hustle, more goals, more visibility equals more fulfilment. But I've seen the other side and it's not happiness that's waiting for us there - it's exhaustion.

What actually creates a good life? Psychological stability. Clarity. Calm. A clear mind that helps you make clear decisions. That's the real flex. People say they want to live "on purpose," but even purpose needs a stable platform to build from. Without clarity and inner steadiness, purpose becomes just another thing to chase.

At the height of my involvement with San Churro, I was a CEO who was expected to be all things to all people – even after I took a step back to raise our eldest child and grieve the devastating loss of our daughter. My marriage eventually crumbled. I *had* to become intentional about building a life that was mine. I am so proud of not losing myself when life got messy, and focusing on raising two emotionally intelligent, hilarious sons who still talk to me.

I walked away when it no longer felt aligned. It takes guts to begin, but it takes just as much to stop. Relocating to the Sunshine Coast to rebuild wasn't a dramatic exit, but a deliberate act of self-preservation that took more courage than any business risk. It has paid off many times over as I have found strength in stillness.

By following my passion for psychology, I have redefined success. Once you understand how to create mental stability, you can lead your own life from a place of deliberate power, not reactivity. I believe psychology is a verb: I'm driven to make it actionable, accessible and fast.

I like to start upstream with tools we can put in place through protective psychology, so you are prepared before you hit the rapids of anxiety or the waterfall of mental illness. I teach people how to swim in the rapids rather than cling to the rocks of addiction, overwhelm and burnout.

No one will believe that I love silence as much as I love a chat, but I am a total "neuro nerd". If you show me a graph of dopamine spikes and behavioural loops, I'll cancel plans. Bonus points if we can talk about decision fatigue over wine.

It's time to stop walking around in the brace position waiting for the plane to crash. News flash! The plane crashed when you were born, now let's walk around the islands and figure out how you want to spend your time in a way that is meaningful for you while on this earth.

KIM MORRISON

ENTREPRENEUR, HEALTH AND LIFESTYLE EDUCATOR, SPEAKER, AUTHOR AND FOUNDER OF TWENTY8

Kim Morrison is a shining example of what it means to live with passion, purpose and perseverance. She has a gentleness that demands to be heard along with an iron will and determination. A world-record-holding ultramarathon runner, five-time best-selling author, motivational speaker and founder of the natural skincare and aromatherapy brand Twenty8 Essentials, Kim is a woman who has turned personal discipline into a way of life and a powerful message for others.

Born and raised in New Zealand, Kim was no stranger to ambition. At just 21 years old, she became the youngest female to run 100 miles in under 24 hours, guided by the legendary Cliff Young. This monumental feat launched her into the world of elite endurance running, setting eight national records and representing Australia at the World Indoor 24-Hour Championships in Milton Keynes, UK.

For Kim, these achievements weren't just about physical strength, her greatest power is her capacity to master the mind. Her belief that success is 90% mental and 10% physical has remained at the core of everything she teaches and lives by.

Kim's passion for human behaviour and natural health led her down the path of perpetual learning, studying aromatherapy, home-botanical therapy, fitness leadership, nutrition, neurolinguistic programming, hypnotherapy and counselling.

Combining her knowledge and desire to support others feel empowered in their own skin, she founded Twenty8 Essentials in 2008. The brand champions the power of self-care and the use of natural products that align with the body's 28-day rhythm. From essential oils to skincare rituals, every product is designed with intention.

Through her sought-after Essential Self-Care Weekends and Self-Mastery programs, retreats, keynote speaking, her series of books and her popular Self Love Podcast, Kim has become a guiding light for thousands around the world who are ready to reclaim their health, mindset and joy. However, this knowledge hasn't just come from courses, institutes and coaches: what truly sets this incredible woman apart is her realness.

As a mother of two and wife to former New Zealand cricketer Danny Morrison, Kim understands the juggle of career, family and personal wellbeing. She doesn't just preach resilience, she lives it. Having lived through the loss of her sister-in-law to suicide, a crushing blow to her family's financial stability in 2009 and personal challenges, Kim is known for her honesty, her heart and her ability to inspire people to rise through adversity. Her ability to integrate self-care into everyday life - and as a resource to overcome life's toughest challenges - has become a cornerstone of her ethos.

Whether she's running impossible distances, formulating healing blends, or standing on stage, Kim Morrison's message is clear: You are worth the effort. Self-care is not a luxury; it's a vital act of self-respect.

'THE RACE IS NOT ALWAYS TO THE SWIFT, BUT TO THOSE WHO KEEP ON RUNNING.'

– ZOE KOPLOWITZ

Serve. That simple word has guided my entire life. It first came from my gentle Grandma Dorothy May, who used to say, "If you're ever unsure of your purpose, just serve." At the time, I didn't fully grasp the significance of that message, but now I live by it. Whether I was feeling lost, overwhelmed or unsure of the next step, I always found clarity through service. I believe I've been guided - by people, plants and purpose.

Both my grandmothers influenced me deeply: Nana Myrtle Rose Millicent with her love for plants and nurturing nature, and Grandma Dorothy with her love of baking, calm wisdom and kindness. I still hear her voice in those challenging moments, gently reminding me that everyone is fighting a battle we can't always see.

Along with the grounding given to me by the women in my life, including my mother who worked hard to give us the best she could, running and being trained by Cliffy shaped me into the woman I am personally and professionally. My ultramarathon years taught me to truly understand and appreciate the meaning of staying in my lane, taking care of myself, pushing through when I least wanted to, leaning into the pain, being more afraid of not finishing than finishing, listening to my mentors and knowing how much it meant to make my team proud.

My journey into aromatherapy, botanical healing and essential oils began with a love for nature's gifts. These oils aren't just physical remedies for things like headaches or colds; they carry vibrational qualities that connect to the soul. From ancient rituals to modern-day wellness, I've always believed that the best in nature can bring out the best in us.

Self-care started as looking after my body, my mind and my spirit. Over time, that practice became a way of *being*. To me, self-love is more than bubble baths and massages; it's about knowing who you are at your core, even when life tests you. And trust me, it will test you.

We all experience grief, pain and failure and I am no different. My ninth year on earth was my toughest; my parents' marriage dissolved, I lost my beloved Nana Myrtle, and I was sexually abused. When I moved with my husband and two children from Auckland to the Sunshine Coast in 2006, we carried the weight of unbearable grief as my sister-in-law had taken her life. Three years later Danny and I lost everything financially and had to rebuild from the ground up and we lost Grandma Dorothy after she immigrated to Australia at the age of 90. Life has thrown me some brutal curveballs, but no matter how deep the lows, I've always believed in rising.

I've learned that strength doesn't come from pretending everything's okay; it comes from allowing yourself to feel it all and still having the courage to move forward. As a teenager, I kept diaries filled with tears and fears, but they always ended with hope. "I guess tomorrow the sun will keep shining," I'd write. And it does. That unwavering belief in light after darkness has never left me. The real turning point came when I stopped resisting the pain and started leaning into it. Through all the personal work, the journaling, the rituals and the healing, I discovered something life-changing: surrender isn't weakness. It's where true strength is born.

The power to overcome lives in how we respond. That's why I created Twenty8, to give people real tools for real-life challenges. Whether through rituals, oils or words, my hope is to support others to reconnect with themselves. The most powerful thing you can do is serve yourself with the same love and compassion you so willingly offer others. That's the foundation of self-love.

WWW.KIMMORRISON.COM

KYM McAULIFFE PHILLIPS

FOUNDER AND CEO OF MOVING MADE EASY, AUTHOR

Kym McAuliffe Phillips is a trailblazer. In the male dominated removals and relocation industry she has demonstrated that success can be achieved with more than just brute strength. With over 30 years of hands-on experience, Kym has used observation, nuance and sheer grit to build on a legacy rooted in her family's iconic business, McAuliffe's Removalists & Storage.

Affectionately known as The Moving Angel, Kym quite literally has moving in her blood and courage in her gut. From an early age, she witnessed her entrepreneurial parents in country Victoria revolutionise the removals space by introducing women into packing and unpacking roles. This progressive step added warmth and empathy to an industry often seen as transactional, and it was an important distinction, one which would inform the trajectory of Kym's later career.

Even after leaving school at 14 to pursue hairdressing, life eventually nudged her back to her roots. A government placement opened her eyes to the widespread dissatisfaction surrounding relocation services. She paid close attention to the feedback pouring in, particularly from women frustrated with cold, impersonal moving experiences. Instead of dismissing these complaints, she leaned in and took notes.

Over time, she unveiled a huge gap in the market for a service built not just on logistics, but on empathy, communication and genuine care. It is this kind of attention to detail and nuanced consideration of a problem that are hallmarks of this hardworking woman's success, and not just in her career.

Kym has learned that her gut is the most powerful tool at her disposal. She ignored it more than once, leading her into two consecutive failed engagements to controlling partners in her early twenties. But the moment she listened, everything changed. She took leave from her job and booked back-to-back Contiki tours through America and Europe.

That single act of daring put her on the path to her husband, Brett, and a life aligned with her truest self. Kym eventually leaned on her intuition and drew on that deep well of courage to launch Moving Made Easy, a business with a clear mission: to make moving stress-free, supportive and tailored to each client's unique needs. She cemented her thought leadership with the release of her book, *Moving Made Easy: The Hidden Keys to an Easy Move,* which was the first step-by-step guide of its kind in the industry.

Today, Kym is recognised as more than a relocation specialist. She is a change maker, industry disrupter, decluttering queen, packing ninja and trusted confidante. Her clients describe her as someone who blends the practical with the personal, offering not just moving services but emotional support through one of life's most stressful transitions.

Whether she's guiding busy professionals with an interstate move or helping a senior client downsize with dignity, Kym does it all with heart. At her core, Kym is committed to bringing back good old-fashioned service with a modern, feminine touch: every move is made easy with her angel magic.

Hot, sweaty and exhausted, I dumped my backpack on the ground and relished the opportunity to take off my muddy hiking boots. I was deep in the jungle of Papua New Guinea in 2015 with my dad, who had just turned 70. The trip was intended to honour my grandfather, who fought in the WWII Kokoda Campaign but tragically died in a car crash when Dad was just nine. I didn't realise it at the time, but this would be a life-changing journey with far-reaching impacts.

Our time on the track coincided with Father's Day, which only deepened the emotional and spiritual experience. Walking that track with my dad was physically and mentally one of the hardest things I've ever done, but it gave me clarity, strength and a deep sense of purpose. That trip wasn't just about honouring the past - it became the spark that lit the future.

I'd always had the idea of starting my own business, I'd even registered the business name -Moving Made Easy - after a light-bulb moment with my husband Brett during one of our little "save our marriage" weekends away. But it wasn't until Kokoda, where I truly pushed myself beyond what I thought I was capable of, that I *believed* I could make it happen.

One night during the trek, I had a vivid dream of my branding colours and felt the business come to life. I returned home with blistered feet, a full heart and a fire in my belly. With just $50 in my bank account, no formal education beyond Year 9, and a whole lot of determination, I started Moving Made Easy.

Breaking into a male-dominated industry hasn't been easy. But I draw inspiration from my mum, who is humble about her role as a trailblazer in the industry four decades before me. She experienced a lot of sexism while expertly running the office and

coordinating operations flawlessly while Dad was out in the field. At 75, she continues to inspire me with her determination to show up at her best every single day: Mum still runs a successful business even though she has a cancer battle on her hands. I aspire to have a drive and resilience like hers in all I do.

There have been plenty of moments where I've wanted to give up in business, especially after a serious fall at a client's house left me with two bulging discs, a dislocated hip and a twisted pelvis. I was told I might never work again, but my husband, who always sees the silver lining, said, "You might not be able to lift, but you can still talk and while you can talk, you can write. The fall's a gift." *You've got to be kidding,* I thought, but it turned out to be the push I needed to finally write and publish my book. That injury didn't end my career; it simply reshaped it.

Running a business isn't for the faint-hearted and every day brings challenges, but I've learned to stay in my lane and trust my vision. Every day, I choose to surround myself with good people, the kind who lift you up, hold you accountable and won't let you linger in a pity party when things get tough. And let's be honest, things do get tough, but that's where the right support and solid systems come in. They help you reset and refocus when life throws curveballs.

Yes, there's still the occasional chauvinist, people spreading negativity about changes to the industry I'm trying to make, even copycats - but I see that as flattery. My focus has always been helping people through one of the most stressful times of their life (yes, a Monash University study backs that up!)

Moving house isn't just about packing boxes, it's wrapped in emotion, change and uncertainty. My 'why' is about making that experience easier, calmer and more human. The rest? That's just white noise.

WWW.MOVINGMADEEASY.NET.AU

HAVE FUN
laugh
love you
CUDDLES
kisses hugs
eat
SWEET DREAMS
XOXO
dance
sing
smile
and be happy

LARISSA SALTON

OWNER AND DESIGNER PHOTOGRAPHER AT LARISSA SALTON
CREATIVE PHOTOGRAPHER, OWNER AND DESIGNER PHOTOGRAPHER
AT HINTERLAND AVANTGARDE CREATIVES, WEARABLE ART CREATOR

"Buy a lottery ticket, you should not be alive." This shocking advice came from the ambulance driver who attended to Larissa Salton following a devastating car crash in 2008. Her daily work commute along Steve Irwin Way to Eden in Glasshouse Country Retirement Village had started out just like any other day, before a young man on his phone driving in the opposite direction veered onto her side of the road. He collected two cars before crashing into Larissa. Her life changed in an instant.

The accident left her with five surgeries, while a two-year recovery forced her to leave her 20-year career as a personal care assistant. However, what could have been a devastating ending became the beginning of a wildly creative new chapter. "My body was broken, but my spirit wanted to fly. I couldn't care for others the way I used to, so I turned that care inward into healing, into photography, into art," Larissa says.

Larissa had chosen nursing as her first career because she didn't think art could "pay the bills", but following the accident, Larissa threw caution to the wind: life was too short to put your passions on hold. Mesmerised by the photographer's skills at her daughter's first birthday cake smash, Larissa picked up a camera and soon her own bold, innovative approach to the artform was turning heads.

She followed the call of her intuition, transforming a collection of Charles Dickens *Reader's Digest* magazines into a dress. Larissa quickly became known for her evocative wearable art. Her sculptural, statement-making garments were made entirely from reclaimed materials (the outfits in these photos were made from doona covers!) Pieces like the Period Queen dress - made from unravelled sanitary products - are bold and subversive. Larissa created this particular dress for a fundraiser with Kotex to raise awareness and funds for Share the Dignity, a charity committed to ending period poverty.

Covid forced a shift in direction for Larissa, fusing photography with her wearable art to create fantastical visual stories. Ultimately, her process is both intuitive and evolving, "Wearable art takes time. You start with a vision, but the garment has its own voice. It teaches you as it forms."

Larissa is a travelling artist who splits her time between the Sunshine and Gold coasts, running photography workshops and creating her award-winning pieces. Her work has been exhibited at Caloundra and Noosa art galleries, on fashion runways including the Australian Wearable Art Festival, Sculpture on the Edge and at community events like the Nambour Show. She's a two-time winner at the Cooroy Body Art Festival and a finalist in the Clayton UTZ Art Awards.

Through years of grief, trauma, and even a narcissistic relationship, Larissa has kept moving forward, always finding beauty in the broken alongside her five children, all of whom have their own creative pursuits.

"Every day I choose to say, 'Today will be better.' I'm stronger, wiser and still growing."

'MAKE YOUR LIFE A WORK OF ART'
– LARISSA SALTON

There is nothing as constant as change, and women cycle through numerous phases, the maiden, the mother, the wild woman and the crone. I am grateful that I have been able to experience all of them in this lifetime. I am at a crossroads again after the passing of my mother, the end of a narcissistic relationship and becoming an empty nester. I have been in the grips of a dark depression, but I have found my way back to the lightness of creativity once more.

I was a creative spirit as a maiden. My mother wouldn't let my brother and I watch TV and instead, she handed us a big craft box and told us to create something and bring it back to show her. If we weren't crafting, we were outside building cubby houses or fairy gardens out of sticks.

Evolving into a mother, practicality took over and I chose a career in health to provide financial stability for the family. In this phase, it took a life-changing car accident to shift me back onto the creative path I was fated to be on. My mother nursed me back to health and my children were my saviours as I got back on my feet and rediscovered my sense of self.

No matter how broken or broke you are, you can always choose to get up and shine. You can make milk go a long way if you add hot water to your weet-bix - if you know you know! Life is your playground - go and play every day, don't say "next week" or "next month" … there is only today.

Enter the wild woman. Once I set my course on photography, I was fierce, determined and inspired by the things most people take for granted. The way the light reflected off the water at a certain time of day, the way spoons could be bent to create a perfect halo to sit atop a model's head, or even the ability for discarded curtains to find a new lease of life as a stunning garment.

The limitless potential of everything makes my head spin in the best possible way, brimming with ideas and possibilities to create something beautiful.

I lost my mother— my anchor — in 2023 but I am so grateful I was able to care for her until she passed away in my arms. While processing deep grief and navigating the awful legal process that comes when a loved one passes, I was also left alone to pick up the pieces after a three-year relationship with a narcissistic boyfriend.

The weight of it all thrust me into a deep, dark depression for almost a year. My creative spark was extinguished and for the first time, I was truly challenged to see the positives in life.

You need to do something for you. The inner voice was loud and clear. After 30 years of lost socks and cut lunches, I needed to centre myself for this next phase of life. I booked flights to Dubai and Türkiye, where I underwent a full body reconstruction. I am so happy with the results as I can now walk and exercise without pain and I feel like a whole new woman.

Now my children are having their own children, I am transitioning into the crone. Imagination and ingenuity are part of my world once more, but I know there is something even more magnificent just over the horizon waiting for me. I am yet to see what form it will take.

My obstacles have been many, but I still get up each day with a smile because there is absolute joy in being a woman and experiencing what it is like to express and explore my sense of self in each stage. It may be challenging at times, but each new day is a fresh page on which you can write your own magical journey.

INSTAGRAM: LARISSASALTONPHOTOGRAPHY

45

LILLIAN MUCHIRI

FOUNDER OF KARIBU LIFE AND RECOVERY COACHING, KARIBU WOMEN'S & CHILDREN'S HOME, CLINICAL NURSE, MENTAL HEALTH SPECIALIST, SPEAKER, BESTSELLING AUTHOR

The gentleness in Lillian Muchiri's eyes contradict each courageous and deliberate step she's made from a lifetime of certain subjugation. Born in Marimanti, Kenya, and raised in a compound with her father, his three wives and her 18 siblings amidst poverty, inequality and cultural silence, Lillian grew up watching the women around her carry immense burdens without complaint. It was a fate that would have been Lillian's had her eldest brother not intervened, working hard to pay for her secondary education.

Falling marginally short of a scholarship to university, Lillian's dream of becoming a teacher or nurse slipped away: the $900 admission letter to enrol was beyond her means. Determined not to repeat the story of many Kenyan women, house-bound, dependent on and obedient to their husbands, Lillian applied for the National Youth Service. If she could withstand the regimented lifestyle and training for 12 months, she could further her education and change her life forever.

It was another male-dominated environment, but Lillian commanded her place, coming second in fitness assessments, like cross-country and health checks. Based in Nairobi at the Kenya Forest Service headquarters, she became part of the uniformed forces tasked with patrolling the national forests; along with a gun, she carried permission to use deadly force to impose the law. She attained a degree in human resources and work with the government payroll, but her world was derailed by an abusive relationship, and she lost everything she owned in a fire.

Life had dealt many blows to Lillian, but there was a second chance; her brother offered to help her migrate to Australia. To leave everything she knew behind, start again on the other side of the world with very little demonstrates incredible bravery. To begin work immediately in two jobs to fund her nursing degree and send money home to her family is a testament to her tenacity.

Lillian's nursing career spanned emergency and aged care before evolving into specialised work in mental health, supported by the master's degree she completed when her youngest son was just three years old. There, she discovered her true calling - supporting people through trauma, grief and psychosocial challenges. She now balances work in Queensland Health with her own business, Karibu Life & Recovery Coaching, helping individuals, many from migrant and marginalised backgrounds, to reclaim independence, resilience and self-worth.

Lillian's mission reaches beyond Australia, and she has returned to Kenya several times with her sons and reconnected with village elders, speaking openly about the mistreatment of women and children - topics once considered taboo. She has purchased land in her hometown and has a vision to create lasting change from the ground up.

Her bestselling book, *Looking Back to Move Forward*, is a courageous reflection on her life. It shines a light on cultural traditions that need questioning, while honouring the strength and stories of the women who shaped her. Lillian's story is about surviving systems that tried to break her and using that strength to build something meaningful for those left behind.

'TOUGH TIMES DON'T LAST, TOUGH PEOPLE DO.'
- ROBERT H. SCHULLER

My village is an arid, cut-off place where clean water, education and safety were luxuries we only dreamed of. We walked seven kilometres to fetch dirty water from a drying river, to drink, wash and use as our means to survive.

My mother was the third wife in a polygamous compound, which meant we often went without. My siblings and I would look for food from the land because there was often nothing to eat. I went to school not for learning, but for the food programs Canadian volunteers provided. That simple boiled maize and milk saved our lives.

Violence and hardship were woven into our daily lives. We were beaten by the headmaster or teacher on duty if we were even five minutes late for school. My mother suffered terrible abuse at the hands of my father and was forced to leave us for months to farm crops. As children, we did our chores, looked after each other and did our best to get through each day.

When I turned 13, I endured female genital mutilation, a 'rite of passage'. Refusal meant rejection from my community. While I was healing from this traumatic practice, the women from our village educated me on how to serve my future husband. We knew no different; it was just the way things were.

I couldn't accept this kind of future. My brother, Michael, also saw more for my siblings and I. He paid our way through school by selling second-hand clothes and tutoring, believing education was our escape. Because of him, I went to high school and eventually Kenya's National Youth Service, something usually reserved for boys. I begged my father to let me try, and when I was accepted, I ran home crying with joy. *This is my chance.*

But it was in the bush - ordered to shoot a man cutting trees to feed his family - that I saw my old life staring back at me. I couldn't do it. He pleaded with me and explained he was forced into illegal logging to feed his family. I understood more than he realised. I let him go with a warning. That moment crystallised who I was - a woman raised in hardship, but unwilling to perpetuate it.

48

When an abusive relationship and a fire in our barracks nearly took my life, my brother fast-tracked an Australian visa for me. With this incredible opportunity, I have done everything I can to build a life on my own terms. I found love, and even though my marriage did not last, I am raising two strong young men who are connected to their culture.

I have found purpose in my career as a clinical mental health nurse, and I use my past to relate to people from all walks of life who have challenges that seem too big to overcome. I show them how anything is possible with the right tools and mindset.

In recognition of how fortunate I have been to break free of the path laid out for me in the village, I established a charity. All my extra funds are channelled here - from sales of my book to fundraising events and even speaking fees from my professional engagements.

Those funds have bought a two-acre block of land; I've already had a 150,000-litre water tank built on it with plans to create a borehole. This will provide fresh water for the village – something we take for granted here in Australia - and ensure future generations in Marimanti can be healthier and happier. I also dream of creating a space where women and men can thrive together and start to challenge some of the outdated cultural practices that minimise women.

I've come far from Marimanti, but I've never forgotten it. My pain gave me purpose and now, my voice is a bridge between those two worlds.

WWW.KARIBUWOMENHOME.COM.AU

49

HOW DO YOU INSPIRE YOURSELF TO TAKE ON A NEW CHALLENGE?

BEC BEAR

Get organised. Make sure I have the head space and resources to succeed. Practice self-care and prioritise my close relationships. Exercise; stay fit. All these things keep me connected to myself and my loved ones. Remember what you loved to do at nine years of age before the creativity was bashed out of you, and hold onto that passion like a dog with a bone. Never give up on it. Living my most inspired life has required my commitment to knowing myself so deeply that I can reject all that doesn't serve me.

BERNI MORRIS-SMITH

Spending time in nature is where I draw so much inspiration. I've learned there is power in being still, which is something I never used to do. When I'm gearing up to do something new or challenging, I take myself away from everything that distracts me and listen to what's going on in the universe. It takes a few days to undo all the noise and then hopefully the crystallisation of thoughts come. Painting also helps restore calm. There is something magical about starting with a blank canvas and creating something that was never there before.

FRAN BLANDON

By sharing my story with others who are having a tough time, I have given them hope. I am living proof that if you remain strong and true to yourself you can overcome anything. I also realised how important it is to practice self-love to understand your worth, but also to show empathy and compassion to others, to offer them the support they need during difficult situations.

JENNY LAWSON

Talk with my team, or my family, depending on the challenge. I'm often the steerer of my canoe, the captain, and am tasked with reading the wind, swell and other teams, while also inspiring my own team to stay motivated for races from 10km to 70km long that can take one to six hours to finish. The "motivational speech" I give my paddling team is similar to the one for my Successful Grants team and is usually more to motivate and remind me to work hard… but it flows to them also.

SANDRA GOULTON

I journal and start writing down what I love. Then I make a start, listen to a podcast, walk, do something for someone else… put a stick it note on my mirror that reminds me "You are Enough!" And don't be afraid to reach out for help.

MAUREEN 'MOZ' MILLER

BEAUTY BUSINESS ENTREPRENEUR, NEUROLINGUISTIC PROGRAMMING PRACTITIONER, TIME LINE THERAPY PRACTITIONER, FOUNDER OF MOZ MILLER COACHING

Moz Miller's life has never followed a straight line. It's been more like a long, dusty, dirt road full of twists and turns, hat changes and reinventions. From one chapter to the next, she has embraced many roles, each one adding depth and purpose to create the woman she is today.

She grew up a horse-loving country kid, the kind who was riding trackwork at stables before school. By the time most teenagers were thinking about exams, Moz had already left school to chase her dream of riding in the big smoke. That dream was interrupted by a broken leg, but if there's one thing Moz has never done, it's stand still for long. Moz collected experiences like most people collect souvenirs.

She spent a year as a jillaroo on a million-acre property, then followed the sun around Queensland. There was property work around Emerald and Springsure, before she was back in Emerald working as a vet nurse. At the Gladstone Alumina Refinery, she was a trades assistant; in Longreach, a nanny. She studied business in Toowoomba but cut her course short to return to Longreach to work at the police station. She juggled her position at the station with work behind the RSL's bar, where she honed her people skills getting to know the locals. Moz then tried her hand at hairdressing, managed a retail store and even worked in the cattle trucking industry.

A stint at Dreamworld on the Gold Coast was followed by a decision in 2013 that would send her flying into the red dirt of Birdsville. Moz jumped on a plane and landed in a road crew contracting camp based in Boulia, spending the next few years working from Birdsville to Bedourie, driving water trucks, road trains and machinery most people only ever see in movies. Across some of Australia's most remote regions, Moz worked, lived and delivered mail.

Burnt out and ready for a change, Moz's intuition was telling her she needed something different. The dirt roads took her to the coast, where she swapped heavy machinery for skin science. Moz studied full time on the Gold Coast and earned the accolade of Facialist Student of the Year, leaving with a fresh lease on life.

With the Outback still in her blood, Moz chose Mount Isa to start her beauty career. She worked in local salons and loved the community so much, she entered and won Mount Isa Rotary Rodeo Queen. A move to Roma followed in 2018 with the second major intuition whisper - to launch her own business. It began as a home-based salon and grew to a thriving shopfront with a growing team.

Moz became a multi-award winner at the 2020 and 2024 Maranoa Business Awards and a finalist in the Australian Beauty Industry Awards in 2024. Despite the outside success, Moz knew something was missing and she began a new type of journey - not to become a coach, but to better understand herself. She enrolled in courses, seminars and workshops as a participant, returning later to volunteer as crew to cement her own learnings, and to support others.

It became clear how transformative it is to truly "know thyself" as Moz says, and she discovered something even more powerful: a passion for helping others do the same. From paddock to polish, Moz's story is a testament to the power of embracing every twist and turn.

'SOME OF YOUR BEST DAYS ARE YET TO COME.'

– MOZ MILLER

Sometimes I feel like I've lived ten different lives in one. I've got my HR licence, open bike licence, machinery tickets, and even started my pilot's licence once upon a time. I grew up a country kid, in love with the land, horses and the thrill of gymkhanas and camp drafts. The dust, the freedom, the early mornings… it all lit something in me that's never really gone out.

But what might surprise people is that I've always had this pull in both directions. One part of me belongs to the Outback with leather boots, grit and big open skies. There is a peace there and a real connection to authenticity that cannot be matched in big cities. The other part? She's all about refinement, self-care, connection and learning. I've lived and worked across the country and no matter the postcode, I've always chased what felt true in the moment.

I guess you could say I've got a gypsy soul, and it wasn't until recently that I appreciated the true power of following your intuition. Believe me, it is never wrong. There have been times when I shut my instincts down, like the time I packed up my Roma salon to move everything to Toowoomba. It didn't feel right, and I knew in my heart that going against that inner knowing would not serve me well. So, I turned around and came straight back. Some people might think that was crazy, but that inner knowing has guided me more than any business plan ever could.

In 2019, I took a chance and went to see Tony Robbins. That event changed everything. Personal development became my next adventure. I dove headfirst into NLP, Time Line Therapy, coaching courses and workshops. At first, I was driven simply to understand myself better. But the more I learned, the more I could see the inner power I always had but never acknowledged.

Something clicked; I saw how much this work helps people because I could see the real-time changes in me. Being brave enough to do the inner work has helped me to heal and truly appreciate that inner strength isn't just about pushing through, it's about presence, peace and purpose. After years of helping people feel beautiful on the outside, I'm ready to walk beside them as they rediscover and nurture their beauty within through Moz Miller Coaching. Real transformation doesn't start with a new lipstick or a fresh haircut; it starts with knowing who you are, what you value and what kind of life you want to create.

Through the people I have met during my own personal development journey, I've learned that change is always possible, no matter your age, your past or your current circumstances. Self-development isn't about fixing what's 'broken'; it's about uncovering the power, wisdom and self-belief that has been within you all along.

I love people. I love hearing their stories, finding the thread of magic woven through their experiences and reminding them of what they're capable of. Whether someone is standing in their power or feeling a little lost, I want to be the voice that says, "You've got this." I want to offer the tools, encouragement and truth to help them rise.

The more I've grown, the more I've seen how limitless we really are when we decide to stop playing small. It's not always easy. Growth requires courage, honesty and a willingness to feel the uncomfortable stuff. But on the other side of that discomfort? There's clarity. There's confidence. There's a future designed on your own terms.

Because if there's one thing I know from all the wild adventures and winding roads I've travelled—it's that we're allowed to change. We're allowed to outgrow old versions of ourselves. We're allowed to start over and when we take those brave steps with intention and heart, we remember just how powerful we truly are.

INSTAGRAM: MOZMILLERCOACHING

MELISSA PAYNE

MANAGER OF STUDENT FINANCE AND SCHOLARSHIPS AT UNIVERSITY OF THE SUNSHINE COAST, JUSTICE OF THE PEACE, VOLUNTEER

Melissa Payne is the epitome of the quiet achiever, the kind of leader who doesn't seek the spotlight but leaves a lasting impact. She has climbed her mountain, and spent more than 17 years working behind the scenes to help others climb theirs. In her role at UniSC, over the past five years alone, she's helped deliver over $20 million in scholarships and support payments to students doing it tough. The parallels to her own courageous journey are stark.

Mel grew up in Toobeah, a remote town in western Queensland with a population of just 45. Ambition often felt like a distant dream, especially when getting to high school meant a two-hour daily bus ride. But she showed up, day after day, determined to make something of herself.

After high school, Mel completed a traineeship and was named Trainee of the Year. It was an auspicious start, but her struggle up the academic mountain had only just begun. Bone-deep grief, the demands of motherhood, financial hardship, full time work and frequent moves due to her husband's army career, meant Mel's qualifications were painstakingly built piece by piece. Over several years, she completed a Diploma of Business, several Certificate IVs, a Graduate Certificate in Business Administration and eventually, a Master of International Business.

Each course gave her a taste of what she could achieve; her confidence grew. She harnessed that drive to succeed; Mel became unstoppable. Every role, from foundation staff member at Fraser Coast Anglican College school, to progressing up the ranks to become Financial Services Branch Coordinator for the former Maroochy Shire Council, was a source of pride for her family.

"When I looked out into the crowd from the Graduation stage, I could see my family, especially Dad standing there with his camera looking as proud as punch. He was just so proud of everything I did, including being the first in our family to go to university. He would always look at me and say, 'Not too bad for a girl from the bush'."

It was only while preparing to feature in *Women Inspired* that Mel realised the significant correlation between her current role at UniSC and her own path with academia. Positioned to help students struggling financially so that they might stay the course and complete their qualifications, was the very support Mel needed to alleviate the incredible stress she faced as a student.

Mel is driven by a deep commitment to making a meaningful difference in the lives of others. With a strong belief in the power of opportunity, she works to create spaces where every student feels valued, supported and able to thrive. Her passion lies in breaking down barriers, particularly for those navigating significant challenges, knowing that even the smallest gestures can spark lasting change. Her quiet strength and unwavering belief in others inspire those around her to believe in themselves, often long before they realise their own potential.

Grounded by empathy, accountability and trust, Mel leads with care and compassion. These qualities have been strengthened through resilience, hard work and a quiet determination to keep going, even when the path was unclear.

Not too bad for a girl from the bush!

'YOU MUST DO THE THING YOU THINK YOU CANNOT DO'.
– ELEANOR ROOSEVELT

There was not a lot to do in Toobeah. I'd be surprised if you've even heard of it. The humble town only had seven homes, a pub and a petrol station that also served as the post office and general store. Kids like my younger brother Danny and I had to make our own fun… and the options were limited. The highlight of our school holidays was going down to the pump hole, which was the local water source, and doing a mud slide that was so brutal it would often rip the bum out of your swimmers. Otherwise, we would ride horses and motorbikes.

Barely two years apart, my brother and I were inseparable. He was my best friend. Everything shattered when the police knocked on the door of Mum's house. I still remember the way the air left the room, how the silence screamed. Danny had been killed in a motorbike accident, and we buried him on his 18th birthday. Nothing prepares you for that kind of loss. Not the suddenness, not the finality, and certainly not the hole it leaves behind.

That heartbreak created a deep shift in me: life suddenly felt fragile and unpredictable. It was something we didn't really talk about as a family, for fear of upsetting each other. So, I held it in. And when you hold something like that in, it finds its own way out. For me, that meant drinking heavily on weekends in an effort to forget, to blur it out.

Eventually, I realised I couldn't continue down that path. I wasn't living. The realisation that I was holding myself back from life was sudden, and it forced me to grow up quickly and reconsider what truly mattered. It gave me a sense of strength and clarity I couldn't ignore, and I knew I couldn't let another moment pass me by.

Even then, I spent years searching for where I belonged. Early in my career, I battled self-doubt, especially without a university degree. I enrolled in study programs time and again, but fear and uncertainty convinced me to walk away before I could finish.

My husband and I went through years of financial hardship, and my heart broke all over again when I had to return to full-time work just four weeks after our son was born.

I was overwhelmed by the fear that he wouldn't know I was his mother, with the daycare staff spending most of his waking hours by his side. The reality was, as a family, we simply couldn't make ends meet without both of us working to support our children.

But the fighter has always been in me, and she reminded me that second chances aren't guaranteed. I stopped waiting for the 'right time' and chose to start pursuing my goals instead.

I went back to study, pushed through the fear, and eventually earned my master's degree while showing up for my family and my career. Holding that degree in my hand in 2012 is a moment I will never forget. It was the tangible proof that I had turned pain into purpose. That journey shaped my resilience, my work ethic, and the deep compassion I bring to every part of my life. There were times I felt invisible or unsure, but I kept showing up.

Despite a less than traditional start to his life, I'm incredibly proud of the relationship I've built with my son, Daniel. One of my proudest moments was sitting on stage in full academic regalia watching Daniel graduate with his Bachelor of Computer Science in September 2024. It wasn't just about witnessing his achievement, but understanding the hard work and sacrifices it took to get there. Now, seeing him pursue a Master of Artificial Intelligence with high distinctions while working full-time fills me with immense pride. Watching him reach his potential is one of life's greatest rewards. Together, we honour my brother every day by always showing up; by living life the way he never had a chance to.

WWW.LINKEDIN.COM/IN/MEL-PAYNE/

MIA BANNISTER

FOUNDER OF OLLIE'S ECHO: PATHWAYS TO PREVENTION LTD,
QUEENSLAND PARTNERSHIPS MANAGER FOR HOMES FOR HOMES,
FOUNDER OF COLLECTIVE TRIBE

For Mia Bannister, the trajectory of her life was a series of thoughtfully placed intersecting lines. Renowned and respected in the property industry as a strategic thinker, straight talker and excellent networker, there were few challenges she couldn't navigate.

She left her hometown of Gympie for Brisbane and began her career in the mid-90s as an executive assistant while studying business at university. Over the years, she carved out a niche in business development, working with architects, builders and project managers, often pioneering roles that didn't yet exist - especially for women in property.

Clever, diligent and authentic, Mia didn't just build projects; she built connections. From parquetry floors to high-level development deals, she became known as the "horse trader of information," with an uncanny ability to join the dots across the industry. Along the way, she raised her son Ollie, who was by her side at meetings and industry events almost from birth. He was, as she says, "the youngest member of the Property Council's Future Directions committee."

But in 2024, those straight lines shattered into a thousand pieces when Mia lost Ollie to suicide after his battle with anorexia. That staggering heartbreak redefined her life. Full-time corporate work was suddenly meaningless. There was only one way to make sense of the overwhelming grief, and she began to channel her innate intelligence, persistence and care into purpose-driven initiatives.

Today, Mia juggles three meaningful roles. As Queensland Partnerships Manager for Homes for Homes, she collaborates with developers and governments to fund social housing through property contributions. Through her consultancy, Collective Tribe, she helps values-aligned organisations build lasting stakeholder relationships through her mantra, "business development is everyone's business."

Most profoundly, she founded Ollie's Echo: Pathways to Prevention, a charity honouring Ollie's memory. Its mission is to raise awareness around eating disorders in boys, something all too often overlooked, and drive prevention through education and systemic change. Mia speaks openly about youth mental health and the dangers of social media.

On reflection, her path has been anything but linear. She's experienced redundancy, the collapse of a 20-year firm and the pressure of balancing purpose with financial reality. But she's also rediscovered her resilience and embraced a vulnerability that is helping others move through grief and mental health challenges to find purpose in their experiences.

Mia is honest about the chaos, "Some days I feel like I'm drowning," she admits. But she's also clear: this chapter is about turning grief into action and love into legacy. Through Ollie's Echo and her continued presence in the property sector, she's ensuring her darling son's voice—his echo—rings hope to young men suffering around the globe.

'KINDNESS IN WORDS CREATES CONFIDENCE. KINDNESS IN THINKING
CREATES PROFOUNDNESS. KINDNESS IN GIVING CREATES LOVE.'

– LAO TZU

Tuesday, January 9, 2024, was the day that changed my life forever. My 14-year-old son and only child, Ollie, took his life at home after a short battle with anorexia.

Looking back, he was in the midst of the perfect storm. His estranged father had reached out to him after four years of zero contact. He was relentlessly bullied at school because of his red hair and had spent 125 days at home. He was also in the grips of an eating disorder due to a new-found obsession with social media reels advocating calorie counting and building muscle mass.

Coming home to find my child dead in his bedroom was something I never imagined I would experience. The grief was unlike anything I could have prepared for. I'm not always okay, and I wish people truly knew that. Every single day, minute, even second is a brutal confrontation with inconceivable heartache and loss. In a world where we're often expected to hide our struggles and put on a brave face, I try to show others that it's okay to be vulnerable and honest about challenges we face.

There are days when it's a constant battle to find the strength to keep moving forward. While I know people offer their clichés with good intentions, the reality is that no one can truly understand the loss of a child to suicide unless they've lived it. It's not about advice or trying to relate in a way that feels comfortable for others. It's about understanding the depth of the grief, the silence that follows and the weight of a loss that words can never capture. I wish people knew that, instead of trying to fix it or offer comfort, simply being there without trying to make sense of the unimaginable, would mean so much more.

In the midst of that unbearable loss, I found an unexpected source of strength through my deep love for Ollie and my desire to honour his memory. I realised that if I didn't do something meaningful with my pain, I might not find a way through it. That's when I began creating Ollie's Echo: Pathways to Prevention. It is a project born from grief, but one that has given me purpose.

Turning my pain into action, raising awareness and advocating for change became my lifeline.

The strength I found came from a place of love and a commitment to ensure Ollie's legacy would help others. It was through this sense of purpose that I found the courage to keep going.

I'm inspired by my son. His courage, creativity and sensitivity continue to guide everything I do. Even in his struggle, he taught me so much about the importance of being seen, heard and understood. I'm driven by a need to change the narrative and challenge the stigma around eating disorders in boys to push for early, compassionate intervention.

I like to think I inspire people every day, through the sheer perseverance to continue on and being raw, authentic and true to myself. By sharing both mine and Ollie's stories, not in a polished or perfect way, I hope to encourage others to do the same. I believe that embracing our imperfections is one of the most powerful ways we can inspire those around us. It's not about having all the answers; it's about showing up and continuing to move forward, even when things are tough.

To fire myself up on tougher days, I remind myself of why I'm doing this work - whether it's for Ollie's legacy or the larger impact I want to create through Homes for Homes or Collective Tribe. I find inspiration in everyday moments - conversations with purpose-driven people, stories of quiet courage and the reminder that even small actions can have a big impact.

WWW.OLLIESECHO.ORG.AU

PAULA WILLIAMSON

LEADING WITH HEART, PURPOSE AND BELIEF IN GOOD.

Paula Williamson's story isn't just about hard work, diligence and climbing the corporate ladder. It's infused with courage, of rising with purpose, staying grounded in values and lifting others along the way. With over 20 years in Australia's banking sector, she is known for her strategic mind, but even more so, her unwavering belief in people and the power of authentic leadership.

Her journey began in the most unexpected way. As a young conveyancing clerk taking a break from university, Paula walked into a Commonwealth Bank branch to complete a property settlement. She walked out with a job interview and soon after, an offer that doubled her salary. "I nearly fell off my chair," she laughs. But she said yes and that leap of faith became the first step in a remarkable career.

From the outset, Paula was driven, but always a team player and while she didn't always see her own potential, others did. Mentors played a pivotal role in her early years, helping her build confidence and a solid foundation in banking and leadership.

One of the most defining chapters of Paula's life came when she returned to work as a single mum to a nine-month-old son. Life had changed and so had her priorities. Determined to create a stable, loving home, she took on a branch manager relief role to get back into the workforce. Her dedication and capability quickly stood out, catching the attention of senior leaders and opening the door to further leadership opportunities.

From there, Paula's career blossomed. She thrived in roles across branch management, compliance and operational leadership and regional transformation. Eventually, she followed a trusted leader to ANZ, where she found her stride supporting the retail network in north and western Queensland, and later in Private Banking with high-net-worth clients. More recently, she's taken on broader strategic and operational roles - always gravitating toward spaces where people come first.

It's not her experience which sets her apart though; it's her beautiful and authentic presence. Whether Paula's engaging with outstanding clients, leading large teams or navigating complex change, she brings care, clarity and action to everything she does. In fact, she's never defined herself by job titles or career labels. She's a mother, a daughter, a friend, a learner and a connector.

Paula is someone who believes deeply in the power of people to grow, to lead and to create meaningful impact in collaboration with one another. As President of the Sunshine Coast Business Women's Network, she is the exemplar. She continues to lead with heart, encourages women to show up fully, follow their passions and give back where they can. And though she humbly refers to herself as "just Paula Williamson," there's no doubt she's making a big difference one conversation, one connection and one courageous step at a time.

'DO ALL THE GOOD YOU CAN, BY ALL THE MEANS YOU CAN, IN ALL THE WAYS YOU CAN, IN ALL THE PLACES YOU CAN, AT ALL THE TIMES YOU CAN, TO ALL THE PEOPLE YOU CAN, AS LONG AS EVER YOU CAN.'

– JOHN WESLEY

I was an accidental banker. The thought of building a career in that realm had never crossed my mind, but life had other plans. An unexpected opportunity came my way, and I took it. Since then, my career has been a combination of consistent hard work, showing up every day and having the confidence to accept any opportunities when they knocked. I certainly didn't map it all out, but I stayed true to my values, trusted the process and let my work speak for itself.

From the moment my son James and I unexpectedly became a team of two, I was determined to build a secure and vibrant life for us. I didn't just want to succeed professionally - I needed to. James shaped every decision I made; I built homes to create an anchor for our family; I worked hard to earn enough to give James access to quality education, sport and travel. Every choice I made was conscious; driven by my undeniable urge to give him the life I had dreamed for him.

At the same time, I never lost sight of the importance of community. When we moved to the Sunshine Coast (my birthplace) in 2017, I had no professional or social network. I would shy away from the camera, but I challenged myself to be seen *and* heard and threw myself into attending events, connecting with people and showing up again and again.

The Sunshine Coast Business Women's Network (SCBWN) quickly became my tribe. I started volunteering, then joined the committee in 2018 and today I'm proud to serve as President. It actually blows my mind that I have been afforded the opportunity to lead a dynamic and purposeful network: if there is any way I can give back to an individual woman, organisation or help the community to grow and prosper, then sign me up!

Whilst you might see a lot of the outward facing stuff with SCBWN, most of the impact of connection is unseen. It is in paying it forward, mentioning other people's names in rooms of opportunity, connecting people who you know can create something wonderful, and welcoming newcomers to the region so they feel accepted and can shine on. The network is genuinely the catalyst for the lifestyle and the friendships that I have, so I'll be eternally grateful for that.

When I turned 40 and James turned 14, I felt an indescribable shift. When he was a baby, I had set myself a goal, which felt heavy at times, that we would be emulating the life I'd had as a child: one of unconditional love, laughter, family, service and prosperity. I threw a party to celebrate and as I looked around the room filled with my loved ones, I realised I had achieved my goal and so much more.

During that pivotal time, the weight of those goals lifted off my shoulders and I could begin to prioritise myself, which was a quiet, but powerful achievement. My very best and very worst quality is that I would always give to others before I gave to myself, so I reclaimed space for myself, focused on my health and lived life more fully as a woman, not just a mum. I became more mindful of where I placed my energy, and this allowed me to experience all types of joy.

The future looks bright, but it is the result of our past. I know for sure that I would never change our past because it has made James and I the strong, capable, kind people who are grateful for everything in life. My biggest achievement in this lifetime will always be James, he is truly the love of my life, and I tell him so constantly.

There were plenty of moments where I doubted myself, but I just kept going. I've built a career, a home, a network of friends and family and a life I'm proud of. I hope that other mums doing it on their own know that it is possible. Set clear goals, work hard, don't apologise. You can do anything you put your mind to: never let a label define you.

WWW.LINKEDIN.COM/IN/PAULA-WILLIAMSON/

DR. REBECCA `BEC` BEAR

PARTICIPATORY ACTION RESEARCHER, POLICY WRITER, HUMAN RIGHTS ADVOCATE

Bec Bear's journey is a powerful testament to resilience, purpose and deep spiritual alignment with what she calls her higher power. A proud Pākehā Kiwi woman, Bec has walked a path shaped by devotion to her whānau and an insatiable thirst for wisdom. Her academic accolades are remarkable, yet for Bec, they are simply milestones in a far greater mission - the relentless pursuit of truth, understanding and a life lived with intention.

Originally trained as a veterinarian, Bec made a brave decision to walk away from the profession she had spent over a decade training and working in. The ethical challenges of vet work in a rural farm setting and the all-consuming nature of the role were involved in her decision to leave the profession, especially when Bec became a mother.

While her first child arrived safely, Bec's second and third children—born within 14 months of one another—were premature and required extensive stays in neonatal intensive care. The medical process deeply challenged Bec's Earth Mother values and set her on a path of personal research to comprehend the impacts of the NICU environment on newborns and their mothers.

With three children born within three years, Bec poured herself into mothering, always prioritising connection to her children and their wellbeing and education while juggling multiple jobs after becoming a single parent. Ready to formalise her passion for understanding the mother-baby bond, Bec returned to formal study in 2015 when her youngest was 12, committing to the four-year doctorate at Victoria University in Wellington. The topic of Quality Improvement for Upscaling Skin to Skin Care of Medicalised Infants tested Bec's limits, but also became one of the most transformative experiences of her life.

Bec went on to apply her real-world research expertise to the field of mental health and suicide prevention, working with victim-survivors of abuse in state care and people with lived experience of mental health and suicide prevention systems. She was the Principal Research Advisor at the Royal Commission of Inquiry into Historical Abuse in Care, worked in partnership with NZ Māori before moving to the Sunshine Coast in 2022, and has taken on a senior researcher role with the Institute for Urban Indigenous Health.

The trans-Tasman move marked a new chapter in her emotional healing journey, one shaped by spiritual practice, writing and deeply personal reflection of the trauma bonds along her maternal line. Bec has three heartfelt goals: to live a sun-filled life, to find a life partner and to publish *Motherless,* the book that has always been in her heart.

Bec's writing talent was first recognised by a university professor who gave her an A+ on an assignment around mammalian physiology. It was a vivid early piece told from the perspective of an egg travelling through a fallopian tube. After interviewing dozens of women for various projects, *Motherless* will be the first time Bec shares her own story.

Inspired by lionhearted women like Oprah, Maya Angelou and Brene Brown, Bec reveals an everyday kind of triumph that shows what's possible when you live in alignment with your values, lead with kindness and dare to rewrite your story.

'TO BE AUTHENTIC IS TO BE TRUE TO A SENSE OF SELF ARISING FROM ONE'S OWN AUTHENTIC AND GENUINE ESSENCE...AUTHENTICITY CAN HEAL TRAUMA.'

– GABOR MATE

was travelling in the UK with my partner when I discovered I was pregnant. While sitting in the bathroom with the positive test in my hand, the initial elation at the realisation of my lifelong dream of becoming a mother was eclipsed by fear of not bonding with my children as I hadn't with my mum.

Being born to my mother tested us both. We have both suffered over the years as I reached so desperately for the love and affection she was unable to give me. You see, she was dealing with her own pain – the result of being forcibly removed from her own mother and suffering at the hands of those who were charged with her care. While she was physically present – her first step towards healing, you might say – she was emotionally disconnected. Something I was determined, even as a young girl, that my future children would never experience. I wanted to truly know them and for them to know that I would have their back for life.

My eldest daughter was my sole focus in life until her siblings came along. When I woke up after an emergency caesarean to see a note on my wristband that read "It's a boy," with my son nowhere in sight, the possibility of a disruption to my bond with him tore at my soul. I fought like hell – through a raging uterine infection and exhaustion – to get myself down the stairs for the skin-to-skin nurturing I knew he needed until I could take him home. I did the same thing for his baby sister. We all have a maternal ferocity lying dormant within us, ready for action. I was the epitome of the most feared mother in the woods - the Mama Bear. I wore my surname with all the strength I could muster as I navigated the nursing routines of the NICU.

There was always hope in my heart that I would be able to heal my own past through the relationships I had with my children. Now they have grown into generous, values-driven, funny and kind-hearted young adults, I am so proud of the bond we have as they forge their own paths.

As an empty-nester, I have time to heal the even deeper wounds I have carried throughout life. The emotional toll of my childhood has made me sensitive, often fearful, and I have had a long history of self-loathing. It takes a lot of energy for me to show up in the world with an open heart, and I work hard at that.

The word *ngākau* means 'heart mind' in Māori and although there have been many times growing up when I couldn't trust the people in my life, I have always been able to trust in following my *ngākau*.

Within this journey of healing, the hardest work has been the inner work. I have moved mountains to be where I am today. I have overcome self-limiting and outdated stories about who I am and what I can achieve, including the oppressive belief that it is selfish to pursue the authentic life I was born to lead. I have always advocated for other people, especially my three children, but I am only a fledgling at doing that for myself.

I embody my best life by practising all that brings me health, wealth joy and beautiful relationships, both with myself and with others. Practically, this means good food, good sleep, quality time with my beloveds, time in nature, time on my own reading and writing. I have a strong affinity for Indigenous worldviews that cultivate relationships with country, kin and community, and living by Te Ao Māori principles keeps me grounded.

Releasing my book *Motherless* will signify the start of a new chapter for me. I have so much to contribute from a wisdom point of view and I would love to stand among the leaders who are lighting the way for women to heal and live in their authentic way.

FACEBOOK.COM/REBECCA.BEAR.5

SANDY BOLTON

INDEPENDENT STATE MEMBER FOR NOOSA

Pity the person who assesses Sandy Bolton's small stature, blonde hair and blue eyes and thinks to themselves: *this should be easy*. There's a power in this woman, a steeliness in her eyes that fights for the best, for many. She has called Noosa home for over 35 years, raised her three children here and built significant and purpose driven careers whilst becoming an integral and much-loved part of the community. Determined and dauntless, Sandy has taken on managerial and consultancy roles with one goal in mind: to create meaningful impact through positive change. She battles tirelessly for a better world, and she does it with a nurturing heart.

Sandy's work has always been rooted in service to people: she has helped both collective and individual efforts, built communities and solved, as well resolved, complex challenges. Her passion for innovation and progress is evident not just in her professional life, but through her extensive voluntary contributions. From her early years on the Isolated Children's Parents Association through to a founding member of Innovate Noosa, director for the four Sunshine Coast Bendigo Community Banks, to sitting on the Community Advisory Council of the Sunshine Coast Primary Health Network, her experiences have been vast.

In 2013, Sandy was elected as part of the bold and visionary team of inaugural councillors to shape the de-amalgamated Noosa Council, narrowly missing out on the council's mayoral position in 2016. Unperturbed, Sandy put her campaign 'hat' back on and six months later, became the first elected Independent Member of State Parliament for Noosa.

A decade on and Sandy continues to serve with unwavering dedication and passion for the community she describes as her 'family' in her 'forever home'. She has championed resource equity for backbenchers and pushed for a vital inquiry into voluntary assisted dying. Determined to show the power of 'doing' versus endless 'analysing,' Sandy funded a successful hospital transport pilot program for residents falling through the 'gaps' to demonstrate how long-standing issues can be addressed. It is now fully funded by the government.

Sandy has served on multiple committees, from Innovation, Tourism Development and Environment, Community Safety and Legal Affairs, through to chairing the Youth Justice Reform Select Committee, and now Health, Environment, and Innovation. Bringing a grounded, thoughtful and independent lens to every discussion and debate, it is her pointed questions which move beyond politicking, and stab at the crux of the matter: what will deliver the best outcome for her community and beyond?

Knowledge and determination; guts and muscle. It's all there as she rolls up her sleeves in grassroots projects, contributes to strategic policy or advocates fiercely for the needs of her electorate, Sandy's legacy *is* integrity, transparency, connectivity and heart. She's proof that one person, driven by purpose and a deep love for their community, really can make a difference.

"NEVER DOUBT THAT A SMALL GROUP OF THOUGHTFUL, COMMITTED CITIZENS CAN CHANGE THE WORLD; INDEED, IT'S THE ONLY THING THAT EVER HAS."

– MARGARET MEAD

My mother was part gypsy, part entrepreneur - a woman ahead of her time. At various times, she trapped rabbits to make stew, netted squid to eat and sell as bait and painted houses in order to follow a late passion for training racehorses. She taught herself plumbing and electrical work to maintain our home, serviced her own car and could dig trenches better than anyone. I never heard her say, "I can't." It wasn't until much later in life that I realised how deeply she shaped my belief that anything is possible.

I was bullied at various schools for being a 'newbie' with an obvious inability to afford uniforms. This led to anxiety, but over the years there was always an unexpected 'someone' to provide comfort or inspiration, whether that be a teacher, new friend or total stranger. Now, I try to be that unexpected 'someone'.

Mum taught me the world was full of opportunity if you got up at dawn and worked hard. Whilst still at school I earned wages as a relief milker and at a chicken hatchery, and then after school in a saddlery and pet store - all to feed my horse and save for my first car. With that car, I launched a business selling discontinued fashion purchased from designer outlets at house parties. I learnt much, including that something heavily discounted can become a liability!

Dreaming of a career in equestrian, I unloaded pallets of beer with football players whilst training in hotels to fund my passion. By 18, I was managing a venue, living on site and experiencing the exhaustion of day-to-day operations. New legislation that saw customer numbers plummet, break-ins and the not-so-wonderful behaviour of intoxicated patrons were quite challenging for someone so young. However, I learned a lot about my own capabilities, resilience and most importantly, people.

After four years of nonstop work, I took a break and began backpacking with $100 dollars in my 'kitty' to get the first bus ticket, working to fund each new leg of the trip. I crewed on a yacht heading across to the America's Cup, and ended up in a tiny community in the Northern Territory when I didn't have enough money to get to Darwin; the bus driver dropped me in the middle of nowhere, but at least there was work!

It was here that I met my future husband. Life shifted to a different pace in a flywire 'home' on a million acres, 44-degree heat and endless dust. Remote life changed me in instrumental ways. I became intensely aware of both the responsibility I had to myself and others, and the need to be self-reliant as well as forming solid relationships, which are essential to survival in the Outback.

It is inspiring what people in remote communities deal with every single day. One woman I met educated her children from the back of a Toyota while she worked with her husband building and repairing fences. She, and all the others I met, never complained. They just got on with it.

A fair proportion of our community may not understand what an MP's week looks like. It most certainly is not a collection of photo ops. For every minute I spend at public events, there's hours of work behind the scenes researching, consulting with stakeholders, writing submissions and speeches. There are Parliament sittings, meetings, travel with my committee for inquiries and many late-night phone calls with residents in distress, responding to social media and even picking up someone who needs a safe bed for the night. True representation is about communities having a voice only aligned to them, not faceless decision makers behind political parties, or vested interests.

There are many parts of my life I have been proud of, especially my children and grandchildren, but I've always lived to serve my community without nastiness or creating divisions and will continue as long as there is breath in my body.

WWW.SANDYBOLTON.COM

WHAT DOES AN INSPIRED LIFE MEAN TO YOU?

KELLY SMITH

It means living aligned with your values, even when it's inconvenient. It's saying no to drama or anything that drains you. It's being deliberate with your time, energy and relationships. It's asking, "What do I *actually* want here?" and making moves toward it, quietly but surely. I listen to Future Me. She's done the thing already. She's calm, a bit cheeky, probably wearing something fabulous. She reminds me I've done hard things before. I'll do them again. Lastly, I think of 20-something me, passport in hand, no safety net. She's my proof.

KIM MORRISON

To be alive is such a gift and something we may take for granted at times. Get up and move your body, that is what connects you to you. Nourish it with good food to ground oneself and take inspired action with daily self-care rituals using essential oils and any other tools to truly honour the amazing vessel you were gifted with. Being aware of your body and health is the greatest gift as it allows you to think and do better. We all know it you can have 1000 problems to deal with, but the moment you have a health problem, you only have one!

KYM MCAULIFFE

It means waking up with a sense of purpose and going to bed with a sense of achievement. It's about doing something that feels fulfilling, something that warms your heart, not because of recognition or reward, but because it just feels right. Real happiness doesn't come from outside things; it starts from within. When you're clear on who you are and what matters to you, you can block out all the noise and stay true to your path. At the end of the day, it's not about perfection, it's about progress. I don't always get it right, but I show up, stay grounded and do the work.

LARISSA SALTON

My affirmation is "make your life a work of art" in every form and in everything that you do, whether it is what you wear, how you present your food, how you keep your home or how you garden. It is all an act of creativity and art. When you can tap into that creativity every single day, your life cannot help but be driven by inspiration. Your life and health are precious. Make it worth living by doing what you want, you need nobody's opinion, you only need to ask yourself *'what makes me happy?'* and do that. Follow your joy.

MIA BANNISTER

To me, living an inspired life means being true to your values, embracing authenticity, and finding purpose in everything you do, even in the small, everyday moments. It's about showing up fully, even on the hard days, and using your experiences—good and bad—as fuel to create positive change in the world. I strive to be transparent about my journey and my struggles, so others know they're not alone in theirs. Living an inspired life is also about showing compassion, not only for others but for yourself and finding inspiration in even the most difficult moments.

SANDY BOLTON

To live with intent. Be kind to all, visualise the life and world you want to live in, and every day do at least one thing that takes you toward that vision whether that be a personal action in your own home or family, and in the community. Be the change you wish to see, smile, and always remember, you are the change through choice. Focus on the positives, reduce the negatives, and breathe!

SANDRA GOULTON

OWNER AND DIRECTOR OF MULTI-AWARD-WINNING MALENY JEWELLERS

Warm, open and leading from the heart, Sandra Goulton is one of Earth's beautiful treasures. While she had no grand life plan as a young girl, her path to becoming the heart of one of Maleny's most beloved businesses seemed set in precious stone from the beginning.

Inlaid with gold, that path was still far from smooth. A tough retail traineeship in Montville left her physically unwell and disillusioned. But Sandra, ever determined, moved on to the Maleny Drapery while also cleaning homes and working casual hours at the Maleny Jewellers. Her only goal at that time was to work hard to save money for her future.

The owner, Barry, was a traditional watch and clockmaker with an old-school way of running things and a loyal circle of customers. In 1997, Barry pulled Sandra aside and offered her a full-time job. Just two weeks in, he dropped her in the deep end, announcing he was heading to hospital: Sandra was in charge. Her knowledge of jewellery? Next to nothing.

"He left me with a copy of *Minerals Rocks and Precious Stones*: that book was the only resource I had. Whenever I was asked a question, I'd duck out the back to find the answer and come back to them!" Sandra laughs, but the memory gives keen insight into her resourcefulness, grit and temerity.

In 2000, Barry handed Sandra a contract, informed her she had what it took to succeed and was buying the business. "I literally signed my life away," she recalls. It was a leap of faith, but Barry saw something she couldn't. With no formal business training— beyond Business Principles at high school— Sandra took the reins and has since built Maleny Jewellers into a treasured community asset.

As luck would have it, her husband Jim had completed a jewellery apprenticeship and was slowly integrated into the team. Sandra modernised the business from the ground up: introducing tills, tracking sales and transforming the shop's layout. The path to business success has had heartbreaking bumps and painful near misses, but Sandra has drawn on her faith, friendship and family to get through. Having an open mind, being a perpetual learner, and surrounding herself with good mentors have also been key to her achievements. Maleny Jewellers has won a plethora of awards (including an Australia Bridal Industry Award) over the past 25 years, but for Sandra, it is the way in which the business has been a platform to help others that brings her the most joy.

Many students have been given a head start in the industry through traineeships with either Sandra or Jim. Whenever someone is in need, Sandra doesn't hesitate to leap into action. Most of all, she loves the intergenerational connections that allow them to provide jewellery for the most precious milestones of many hinterland families– *and* a sneaky heads-up on pending proposals in the community.

While she is partial to sparkly things, there is no doubt Sandra's warmth and tenacity have made her not just a successful businesswoman, but a gem of the Maleny community… one with a true heart of gold.

'YOU DEFINE YOUR OWN LIFE. DON'T LET OTHERS WRITE YOUR SCRIPT.'
— OPRAH WINFREY

was just an awkward Year 11 student in Maleny High's art room when it happened – I met Jim Goulton. We had an instant connection and in the first phone call he asked me out, he ended the call with an, "I love you!" That bold declaration set the tone for everything that followed for us; love first, fear second.

Although I lived and worked in the hinterland while Jim was based in Caloundra, where he completed a jewellery apprenticeship after we graduated high school, we stayed together. By 1997 we were married and then life really kicked into high gear - three years later we'd bought our first home, I'd bought a business, and I was pregnant with our first child. Baked-bean dinners were a thing, and I was always relieved when our parents would offer to have us around for a meal because then we could eat well.

Jim and I found our synergy through distinguished roles in the business. He is the creative mind who designs and fills the store with unique pieces, while I work on the business side to keep things running (and keep Jim from overspending on his masterpieces!)

When our firstborn son Macale arrived, I slung him into a backpack to take him to our store at The Riverside Centre. The surrounding businessowners adopted him instantly and everyone called him "The Riverside Baby". That village spirit kept me going when we were sleep deprived *and* putting our stamp on the store.

We modernised fast and established a good rapport, but progress came with some punches. Break-ins and rising costs pushed us to hire a "marketing guru" who promised balloons, an emcee and instant riches. Instead, he left us drowning in debt.

I felt physically ill not knowing what to do and after crying in the shower in a foetal position, I pulled myself back together, picked up the phone to my closest suppliers and shared the truth of what had happened. When we were met with kindness and a willingness to help us to recover, I had never felt so relieved and grateful for the people we had surrounded ourselves with. That grace gave us oxygen.

I burst into tears when our youngest, Seb, was diagnosed with autism, because I had no idea what it was or what it meant for our boy.

Family has always been our number one priority, so we hired a store manager. I was still involved in the business, but in a smaller way so I could support Seb. He is now thriving as a young adult working at Australia Zoo while Macale is a successful carpenter and our daughter Angelina is flourishing as a station hand in NSW.

A quarter of a decade on, and Maleny Jewellers is still small by choice, but being self-aware has helped me understand when I need to temporarily pull back, so I do not burn out. My best friend from preschool, Michelle Hughes, is the perfect reset buddy. We holiday together, share the load of parenting and support each other; she is a rare and precious gem.

I often get asked how Jim and I manage to live, work and dream together after all these years. Honestly? We pray, we laugh, we walk the hinterland when days get heavy and we still say, *"I love you!"*

It was those three little words that started this life-long journey for us, and I am eternally grateful that I met my forever person in what would otherwise have been just another high school class.

WWW.MALENYJEWELLERS.COM.AU

SHARON FULWOOD

FOUNDER OF THE QUEENSLAND REGIONAL DISABILITY EXPO AND SPINNERS TOURNAMENT

Sharon Fulwood's journey into advocacy and events wasn't something she mapped out, it unfolded through a life lived with grit, heart and purpose.

Back in 1988, Sharon was part of the Miss Australia Quest, raising $25,000 for what's now known as CPL (Choice, Passion, Life). At the time, she had no idea how deeply connected she would one day become to the disabled community.

By 1996, she was the proud mum of two boys with different challenges. Her eldest Jake had spina bifida and her second son, Ryan had Autism Spectrum Disorder (ASD) and Attention-Deficit/Hyperactivity Disorder (ADHD). In 1999, her daughter Emma was diagnosed with bacterial meningitis at just eight days old. Later in life, Emma would also be diagnosed with ADHD and anxiety disorder. Raising her beloved children led to many personal experiences that shaped Sharon in ways she never expected.

In 2007, Sharon helped found the Suncoast Spinners Wheelchair Basketball Inc. and went on to run the annual tournament for 12 years completely as a volunteer. The longevity of the sporting association, which continues to thrive, is a testament to her quiet confidence and passion. It also became a sport in which her eldest son Jake excelled as a competitor on the global stage.

Sharon returned to TAFE in 2016 to study event management and ended up completing 400 hours of volunteer community access work – four times the required amount! It was during this time she discovered her love for expos. She volunteered at several, and when given the chance to run one as part of the Police and Emergency Services Games, she found her calling.

But despite her skills and drive, finding paid work post-study proved impossible. "I couldn't even get a call back," Sharon recalls. At 47, she found herself stuck; qualified but overlooked. Frustrated, she finally said, "Stuff it, I'll start my own business."

With the National Disability Insurance Scheme (NDIS) rollout looming, she launched the Sunshine Coast Disability Expo in 2018. It was a success, and with the support of a business coach and a few sponsors, Sharon expanded fast. Within 12 months, her one expo grew to six, evolving into what's now the Regional Disability Expo (RDE), serving seven regions across Queensland.

Personally, Sharon has weathered many storms, raising children with complex needs, managing her own mental health, and almost losing her business during COVID. But her lived experience as a mother navigating the disability space is what drives her to help other families avoid the isolation and lack of options she once faced.

Sharon's story is proof that every setback can plant the seed for something bigger. As she says, "every step – no matter whether it is forwards or backwards – is still a step in the right direction."

'ALWAYS REMEMBER YOU ARE BRAVER THAN YOU BELIEVE, STRONGER THAN YOU SEEM, SMARTER THAN YOU THINK AND LOVED MORE THAN YOU KNOW.'

– WINNIE THE POOH, A.A MILNE

---

will never forget the phone call I received after my 18-week scan. I was excitedly anticipating the arrival of my first child in 1995, but the sonographer had a blunt message, "Call your doctor, there's something wrong with your baby." *Whoa.*

My husband was working away at the time, and I was dumbfounded. *Maybe I'm having conjoined twins?* My head spun as I thought about all of the worst things possible, every moment of every day for two weeks during the excruciating wait until my specialist appointment.

He was oddly excited to inform me our baby had diastematomyelia. "There will be a lump the size of a pea on his back, but there will be nothing wrong with the baby." Follow-up scans found bub was breach, so I knew I was in for a c-section, but otherwise there was nothing of concern.

When Jake arrived, the cord was wrapped three times around his neck, but I already had a team of paediatricians in the room to care for him. I overheard one say, "That's spina bifida if I've ever seen it!" Because Jake had a closed lesion (normal skin) over his spine, he had an MRI, he was swaddled, and I was told to "treat him like a normal baby" and sent home.

I had no idea was spina bifida was, so I was clueless as to why he was crying all the time. It took me eight weeks to find the Spina Bifida Association and I started getting some answers. Jake had his first major operation – a detethering of his spinal cord – at six months old.

People rarely talk about the grief you go through as a mother when your child is challenged with disabilities. I had seen parenthood as a rosy experience and to see how different my experience was to friends who were having children at the same time was tough.

Jakey is a fighter, and we were in and out of hospital with him until he was 20 years old. He's pretty inspirational, but then again, I'm a bit biased. His siblings had their own unique challenges and my goal in life was to raise them so they could have an equal standing and the skills and abilities to live independently.

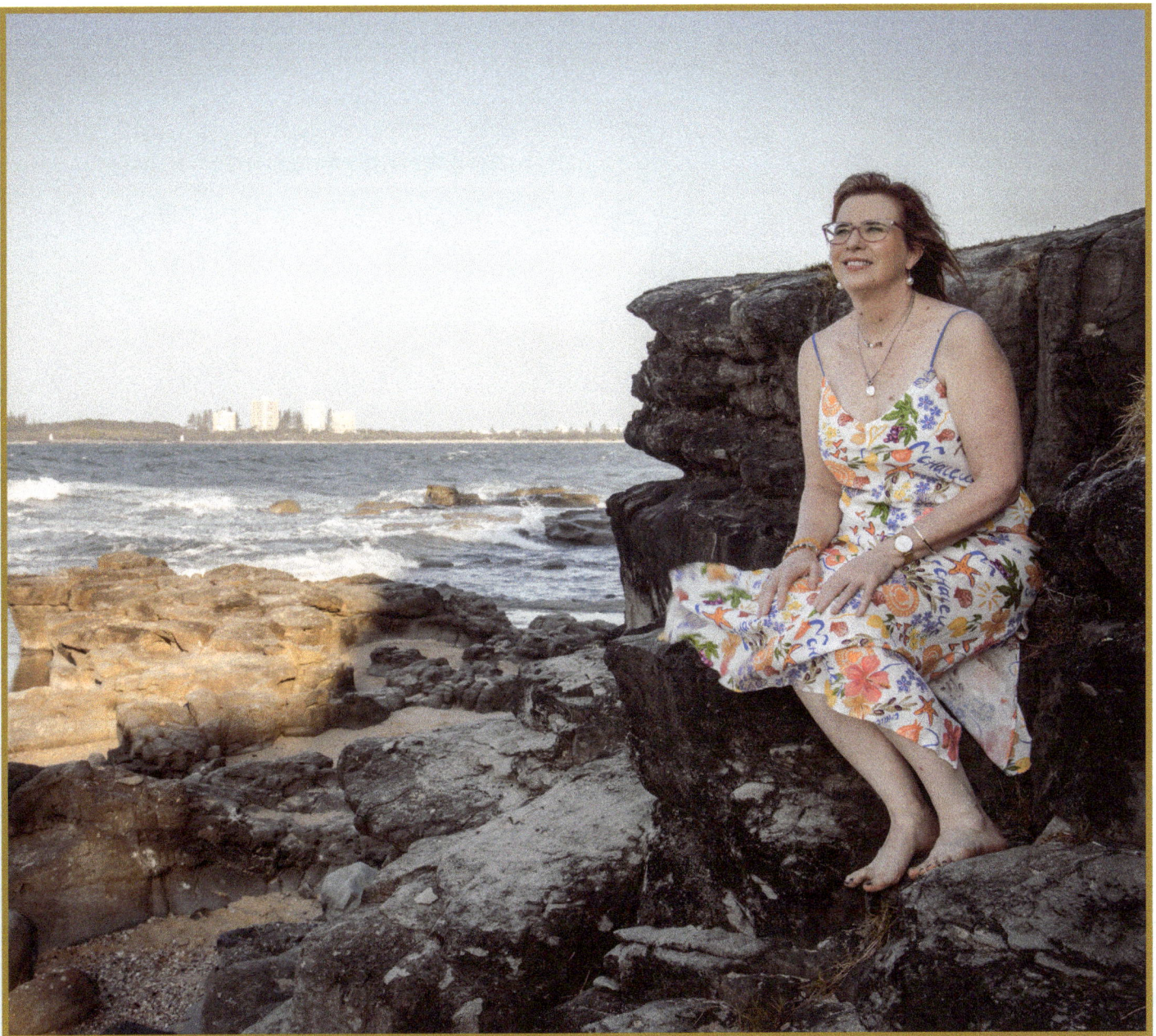

I didn't even know what advocacy was – I simply lived it. But there were times when it all got a bit much. I battled with depression for 14 years, feeling completely overwhelmed and highly emotional, wondering if there was something wrong with me because I couldn't cope with the multitude of medical appointments, hospital visits and day-to-day life.

Reaching out for help through my doctor changed the course of everything. "Thank God you asked for help," he said. He could see I was struggling, but I had to muster the courage to see that I wasn't managing and needed support. I realised that if I opened up to the people who already surrounded me with love and support, they could do even more to help me stay on an even keel.

This ethos is the underlying driver for the Regional Disability Expo (RDE). We don't know what we don't know, and I love nothing more than to see other parents and caregivers overcome that sense of overwhelm because they can arm themselves with knowledge and access services they never knew existed before they walked through the expo doors.

I know my children are amazing advocates for themselves and my mission is to empower people from all around Queensland with the tools they need to advocate for themselves and their loved ones. RDE creates a ripple effect because they pass that knowledge on to those in their circles and it has been an immense source of pride to see that exponentially grow every year.

STACEY McCRAY

SOCIAL CONNECTOR, QUANTUM AND INNER GROWTH COACH, MC, RADIO PRESENTER, COMEDIENNE

Stacey McCray is a woman imbued with vivaciousness, intelligence and determination. Combine that with her insatiable love of learning and curiosity, and it's no wonder she's a success magnet. Known as a "Strategic Connector," Stacey's ability to spot the next wave of opportunity and dive in headfirst has defined her dynamic professional life across three distinct careers. Now she's preparing for a fourth, and it is unfolding as the most authentic one yet.

Stacey was drawn to the emerging merchant banking sector in the 1980s. This signalled the start of a 30-year career in financial services, in which Stacey cemented a reputation for strategic insight, global relationships and people-focused leadership. In 1994, the world of wealth management captivated Stacey, and she built a high-net-worth advisory practice specialising in serving Australian expatriates and international clients, particularly from China. Her collaborative style meant she often worked at the intersection of banking, legal, migration and international tax advisory. That East-West bridge became the cornerstone of her third chapter as an AusAsia business consultant, leading delegations to major forums in Hong Kong and hosting inbound groups looking to build trusted cross-border relationships.

While thriving professionally, there was a misalignment within. Stacey had dedicated her life to delivering results and serving others, neglecting herself in the process. Through Centred Meditation in Sydney, Stacey took the courageous step to the left of centre, and embarked on a path that focused on inner growth, childhood reflection, clearing emotional blocks and stepping into a more aligned future self.

Now, having navigated market booms, global financial crises and a massive personal reinvention, Stacey is tuning into a different kind of currency: wellbeing. A self-confessed "course junkie," Stacey immersed herself in wellness training, meditation, inner growth coaching, positive mental heatlh and energetic healing modalities.

Manifesting a dream to live by the beach, Stacey relocated to Noosa and set down strong foundations for her next season of life. Within days of arriving, she went to Meetups, community and business events. Aware she wanted more fun in her life, Stacey set up the Noosa Social Connections and Noosa Wellbeing Experiences to draw like-minded people into her social network. She is living proof that wellbeing opens the door to a more connected and joyful life!

Stacey has become a familiar voice on Noosa.Radio, hosting The Long Lunch, Making Tracks and Drive Time and her dulcet tones are often on the microphone as MC at events across the Sunshine Coast, including Talk With Wisdom, AIR Noosa events, LNP forums, International Women's Day, and wellness panels.

Known for her vibrant energy and down-to-earth presence, Stacey has a gift for creating elevated, welcoming spaces where people feel safe to share and shine and is taking that to the next level as a qualified Quantum and Inner Growth Coach. She's learned that when you live in alignment, the right people, places, and moments always appear. It's not about chasing the next thing. It's about creating space for what's already waiting.

'FOLLOW WHAT FEELS LIGHT – IT'S YOUR SOUL SAYING YES.'
– STACEY McCRAY

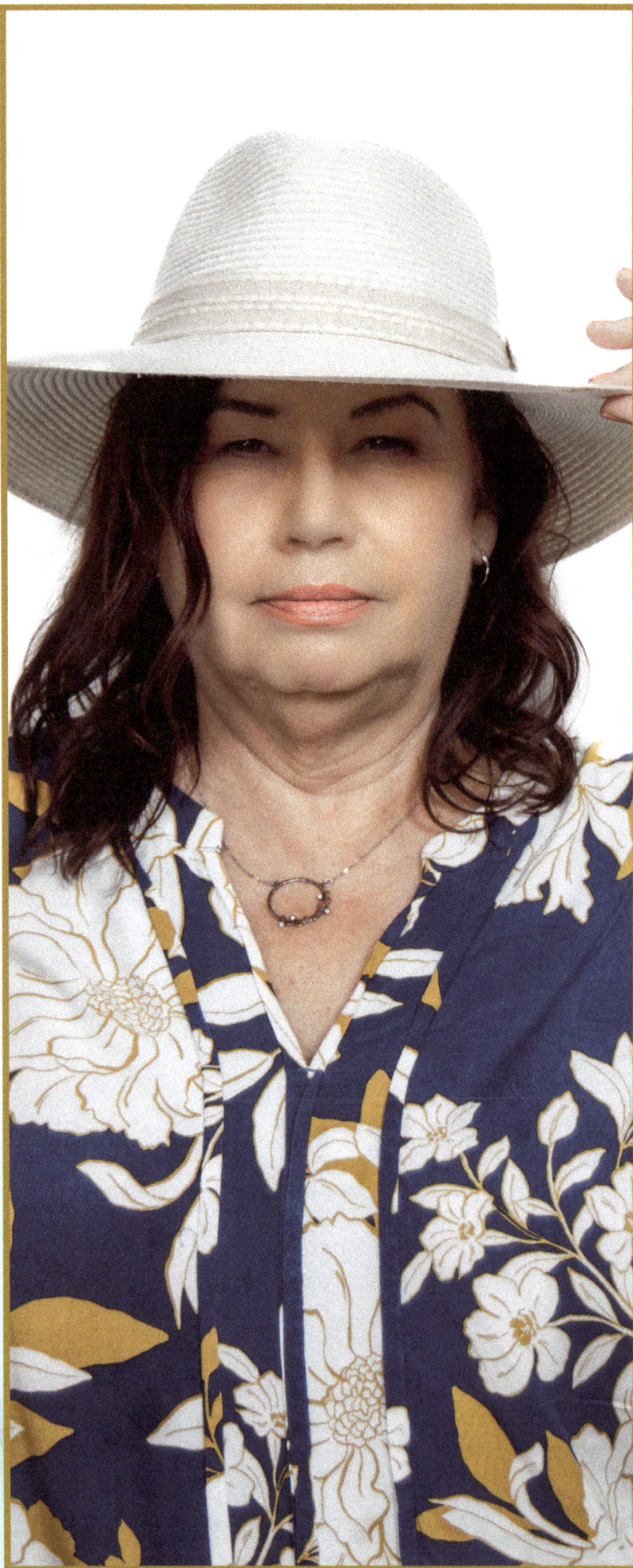

When the clock ticked over on my 60th year on this earth, I had one of those "I can't believe I'm here" moments. I hosted a party as a bold declaration that I was moving into the next phase of my life following a series of life events that collided in the worst possible way 10 years earlier.

They call it a lifequake - a seismic shift that turns your world on its head. Mine ripped through every part of my life and I left my career, marriage, family home and beloved dog while also losing my mum. It all unraveled at once. When the ground finally stopped shaking, I was left standing in the rubble, asking the question: *Who am I now?*

On the outside, I was the high-achieving professional, known for my capabilites and authority. I had it all, plus a house by the beach, which had been a future retirement strategy from wealth generated by following the same processes I had been advising my clients on for decades. But I no longer felt connected to any of it because I had lost my identity in the pursuit of it all. I'd been strong in business, but had lost my personal power.

That was the turning point. Having had coaches and advisors in business, I engaged a Soul Coach to work through the Wheel of Life and realised my scores were alarmingly low when it came to health, fun and relationships.

I no longer wanted to set goals, I wanted to find new hobbies and create habits that grounded me in healthy routines. I studied holstic modalities, unpacked childhood patterns and worked through trauma I hadn't even known I was carrying. I went from finance to full-blown self-exploration.

I found my voice again through comedy, performing five-minute sets in pubs, joking about dating after decades of being "off the market" and decoding the modern world of "FWBs" and unsolicited eggplants. I also found a new body confidence through burlesque dancing. Each time I followed my curiosity to try something new, I found another piece of myself.

I traded hustle for healing and swapped the corporate treadmill for the spiritual path. The stress of maintaining VIP status melted away through barefoot walks on Sunrise Beach with my beautiful furry companion, Jaxon.

I've rebuilt a life grounded in authenticity, community and joy because I gifted myself the space to grow, reflect and reconnect with who I truly am.

Today, I'm no longer trying to be *someone*… and guess what? That surrender of control and shift into a place of alignment led me to a very special someone. Paul is a conscious energy healer who entered my life because his grounded presense resonated so deeply with my way of being.

As qualified Quantum Coaches, we are looking forward to seeing what evolves through conscious connection and deeper energy integration. When you do the inner work, your presence uplifts others and strengthens the communities you are part of.

I sit every day in gratitude that my lifequake didn't destroy me; it revealed me. Now I am passionate about helping people to reveal their true selves through vulnerable conversations. When they feel supported enough to bravely step out of the comfort zones that have kept them trapped for far too long, magic happens.

I turned fear of the unknown future into excitement, because I'm consciously creating it. You also have the power to choose your next chapter, no matter where you are in your story.

INSTAGRAM: STACEYMCCRAYCOACH

STACIE LUSINS

FOUNDER OF BEAU'S PLACE, COUNSELLOR, NEUROLINGUISTIC PROGRAMMING MASTER PRACTITIONER, TIME LINE THERAPY MASTER PRACTITIONER

One in four women will lose a pregnancy, yet the silence around that heartbreak is almost absolute. Stacie Lusins decided the hush had to end.

Stacie had already endured more loss than most. Her grandmother passed away in 2020; exactly three months later she lost her dad. In 2022, her aunty passed and five months after, she lost her unborn baby at 14 weeks gestation. Stacie and her husband Geof named him Beau in honour of Stacie's late uncle, who had passed before she was born.

The couple initially felt isolated in their grief but soon found many friends had experienced a similar trauma. That realisation lit a fuse in Stacie. *If grief could fall this heavily on so many women, why isn't there a place designed entirely for them?*

Determined to create purpose from her experiences, Stacie drew on deep wells of courage and a vision of the blueprint for Beau's Place emerged from the wreckage of her heartache. It would be a Sunshine Coast hub offering community meet-ups, trauma-informed counselling and personalised strategy tool kits to help people who have experienced loss as well as carers of loved ones with chronic mental-health conditions. The concept is intentionally gentle: no fluorescent waiting rooms, no clinical language, just conversation and connection.

Launching a charity while grieving felt audacious and Stacie battled a constant inner whisper: *What if nobody needs this?* The doubt lingered until she tested the idea through conversations. With each connection, it became clear that a hidden community of silent anguish was ready to be seen and heard. Her nomination for a Sunshine Coast Biosphere Community Award soon followed - a jolt of validation that still makes her emotional.

Stacie's credibility comes from lived experience and relentless curiosity. She devours grief-research podcasts on her daily walks and leans on mentors inside and outside the health sector. Family steadies her; music lifts her on rough days. And when the weight of grief returns, she picks up the phone to call her closest supporters, modelling the very vulnerability she asks of others. In bearing the ultimate heartache, Stacie remains selfless and determined.

Since its launch on March 4, 2024, one day after what would have been Beau's first birthday had he been born on his due date, Beau's Place has run monthly yoga circles, bereaved Mother's Day events and private sessions for couples preparing for another pregnancy after loss. Participants leave with practical coping plans, as well as a crucial new contact in their phone for someone who *gets it.*

Long-term, Stacie wants to normalise conversations about miscarriage and medical termination the way breast-cancer advocates have normalised self-checks. She's lobbying for the implementation of greater empathy in the medical space for couples who experience pregnancy loss and workplace bereavement policies that recognise pregnancy loss.

"If the next woman who hears the words 'no heartbeat' already knows Beau's Place exists," she smiles, "then Beau's short life will have changed hers… and that changes everything."

'I AM MADE OF ALL THE DAYS YOU DON'T SEE, NOT JUST THE ONES YOU DO.'

— JAN FRODENO

The high of having a successful 12-week scan quickly evaporated when we had a follow-up call the following day. "It looks like one of the baby's arms is a little bit shorter, you need to have another scan."

As any mother knows, so much hinges on that first trimester scan and I flew into a panic. At the next scan, the sonographer was matter of fact when she said, "Well yes, one of the arms is shorter and the heart is also in the wrong place, so you're probably just going to have to terminate." I was sobbing hysterically. In the blink of an eye, we'd gone from thinking there might just be one problem to the blunt suggestion that there was no way forward for us.

Another scan at the hospital was even more traumatic. The male sonographer was running through the vital organs. "Kidneys look great... liver looks great..." *Maybe it will be okay!* "Hang on, yeah, the heart is in the wrong place... oh and there's only one lung. No one's ever survived with one lung." Once again, the delivery was terrible, but the outcome was clear, our much-wanted baby would likely not make it to term.

The rest of the process wasn't much better. Medically, the team were superb, and we were well taken care of, but everything was so matter of fact, almost casual: there was little empathy. Our midwife was an angel as I naturally birthed our little boy. Our Beau. But the wider system failed us. We were not offered a plan for support and the list of numbers provided to us led to numerous professionals who were fully booked and unable to help us.

Lucky seems like an odd word to use, but I was lucky in many ways; my husband is the kindest soul I know; my family wrapped themselves around us; and, because I'd already lost so many close family members, I had a grief counsellor on speed-dial. We were lucky to have all of that support: so many don't.

Even then, there are moments when it all gets too much. Grief is not linear, but it *is* highly unpredictable. When I see a child around the age Beau would have been, it can bring a smile to my face or send me into an emotional spiral.

That gap in the medical system - the silence, the awkwardness, the absence of practical help - became the catalyst for Beau's Place.

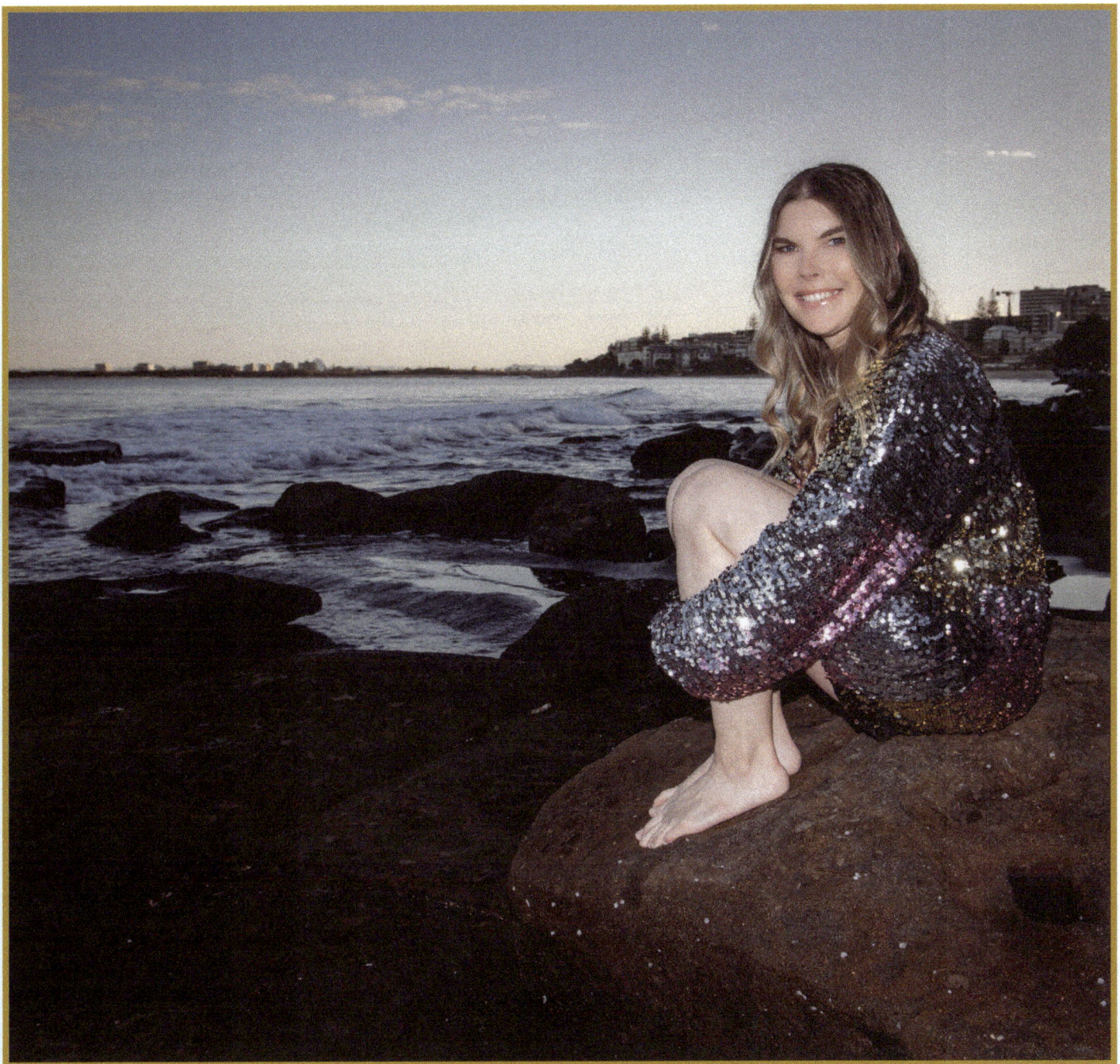

The community is growing and already having an impact. My wish is for the next couple to hear compassion instead of cold facts, the next sonographer to have the right training to deliver news with empathy, and a loved one will know how to have open conversations and offer support without the well-meaning clichéd phrases that often cause more upset. My major goal is to have a trained Beau's Place advocate attached to every maternity ward, much like a McGrath Foundation's breast-care nurses, but for pregnancy loss.

Every day I wish Beau was here with us in the way we'd imagined, but he is out there now, his influence perhaps even more powerful. I take comfort in that.

While trauma has an impact – we can't pretend otherwise – it doesn't have to define you or what the rest of your life looks like. You can come out the other side. You can find meaning. You can find joy - yes! You *are* allowed to feel happy again without feeling guilty about it. You can find hope and new ways to fulfil yourself. Your life will be beautiful once again. You don't have to walk it alone.

WWW.BEAUSPLACE.COM.AU

YVONNE PURVIS

LIMITLESS ENTREPRENEUR, IDENTITY ASCENSION TRANSFORMATION MENTOR

Yvonne Purvis built her first million-dollar business at 28, living a life of freedom, luxury and purpose. She had an innate connection to flow and had the mentors, mindset and momentum to match her success. But after the Canadian-born powerhouse married a man in far-flung Australia, that connection slowly withered, and her true self faded until it was lost altogether.

After years of giving to everyone else, believing the repeated lie that she was 'too much', and ordered continually to dull down her spark, Yvonne felt invisible and disconnected from the strong and assured woman she once was. The real 'her' had been goaded into obscurity.

When her marriage ended, it became more than a divorce - it was Yvonne's wake-up call. She stood at a crossroads with a clear decision ahead: continue living a story that no longer fit, or boldly write a new one. Yvonne chose herself: her vivacious, connected, determined self.

Ignoring the advice of the controlling solicitors tasked with the divorce proceedings, Yvonne relocated from Newcastle in New South Wales—a place she never truly felt settled—to the sandy shores of Noosa in Queensland. The move was both her physical and emotional transition into a new chapter. "Crossing that border with my dog, Sasha, I broke down in tears. It felt like arriving home; not just geographically, but within myself."

It was a soul-level declaration: *I'm ready for more.* That courageous leap of faith made space for a new, elevated version of herself and her business, one completely aligned with her passion and purpose. She learned that transformation begins with a decision and power comes from within to match that energy. The past, the titles, the circumstances - none of it defines you. What matters is the story you choose moving forward.

The result? This vivacious woman has created a movement, helping women rewrite their stories, to break through limitations and live with confidence, clarity and freedom. Her deepest pride isn't just in rebuilding her life, it's in witnessing women rise into their own power.

Yvonne knows from painful experience that in the darkest moments in life, no matter what your age, there is always an opportunity to learn and grow. "The key is to ask yourself: What did I learn? Then, take that next small step toward rediscovering yourself," she says.

As a transformation coach and online CEO, Yvonne helps women across the globe step into their next-level selves by reminding them that they already hold the power to rebuild the life and business they desire, they just have to remember how influential they really are.

Her work blends identity elevation, wealth embodiment and self-leadership to create lasting, aligned success. It's not about surface-level change, it's about activating true transformation.

"Your past, your relationships and your circumstances don't determine who you are. The only thing that defines you is the story you choose to tell about yourself, and that story is always yours to rewrite," Yvonne says.

'A WOMAN'S INTUITION IS THE MOST POWERFUL HEALING FORCE KNOWN TO HUMANITY.'

— YOGI BHAJAN

Sitting cross-legged on the top of a hill alongside a Buddhist monk when I was 12 years old, I felt like I was home. I always felt different, like there was an energy around me the kids at school just couldn't connect with. Like I was meant for great things.

School was never easy for me. I was creative. I loved dancing. I loved acting. That's where I came alive. The school system felt too academic, too boxed-in for the kind of big dreamer I was. Thankfully, I had an entrepreneurial dad who showed me that I could create *anything* I wanted. That planted something deep in me, a knowing that I was meant for more. And my mum? She was always there, doing everything she could to support my dreams and let my soul lead.

Not long after leaving school in Year 11, I auditioned for *A Chorus Line* and got the role. This was the start of my first career. I danced professionally for over a decade before resetting my compass in the direction of event production. I paid $10,000 for a marketing package to establish myself: I had unwavering faith it would work. I was manifesting and tapping into the laws of the universe before I even knew what they were. In a few short years, I had a million-dollar business, and it was effortless.

I was swept away by a handsome and charming Australian during a luxury holiday and for the first time, I ignored my intuition. I decided to move from Canada to his home in Newcastle, Australia and we were married. The first few years of my marriage were tough. There was this constant push for me to be someone I wasn't, and deep down, I knew it. The signs were there early on, but I didn't want to see them.

I spent the majority of our 25-year marriage in doubt, lack, and low self-esteem that consumed me until I no longer recognised the woman in the mirror. The powerful, self-assured entrepreneur had faded out of existence, and I was a shell of myself as I lost my business, my confidence and independence. His criticisms replaced the inner knowing that had never steered me wrong.

I was trapped in a life that didn't fit and after the marriage ended, I had to break free from the version of me that was stuck, unsure and afraid to claim what

I truly wanted. I had to shift my identity; release limiting beliefs and fully step into my power. When the time came to rebuild professionally, I had to trust myself on an entirely new level.

Just as I was beginning to write my book and reemerge from my cocoon, I pulled a tarot card that read *The Crumble,* and I feared everything I had worked hard to rebuild was going to fall away once more. But when I listened to my intuition, I realised it signalled that I was on the cusp of the biggest transformation of all; my old identity was shedding to make way for the next-level Yvonne. Sometimes, what feels like a breakdown is actually your breakthrough.

I am most proud of the woman I've become. I've completely rewritten my story, choosing confidence over fear, abundance over limitation and have created a life and business that reflect my highest vision. It was a rebuild not only from the ground up, but from the inside out.

I'm proud that I took the risks, made the bold moves and trusted myself even when the path was uncertain. And most of all, I'm proud of the impact I've made in helping women step into their power and their identity, and to remember who they are–powerful, capable, magnetic–and rewrite their story from that place. To choose themselves. To create freedom, financial independence, and lives that feel deeply aligned. Watching women come home to themselves, rise in their business and receive the abundance they deserve lights me up every single day. Because everything changes the moment you choose *you*.

WWW.YVONNEPURVIS.COM

97

WHAT ADVICE WOULD YOU GIVE WOMEN SEEKING INSPIRATION?

CHRIS CHILDS

Remove the limiting self-beliefs collected from childhood: when you free yourself of that, you will find a totally new world waiting for you. Discover the power of positive thinking; not the toxic kind where you ignore life's ups and downs, but the amazing kind when you can find something good in every situation.

DR. KAREN SUTHERLAND

Become still and look within. It has always been with you. You create your future now. Take joy in the simple things: nature, your favourite food, laughing with your friends. It's the tiny moments that create a big life.

MOZ MILLER

The truth is you don't have to be special to be successful, you just have to be what most people aren't: consistent, determined, willing to work for it, no shortcuts, integrity, purpose, determination and disciplined. It is the combination of all those things that are the building blocks to being a champion in life.

PAULA WILLIAMSON

Be really honest with yourself about who you are, but more importantly, what's important to you. I think sometimes as women we get caught up in societal expectations or what we think we're *supposed* to be doing or where we think we *should* be. You just need to be honest about what is important to *you*. When you get really clear on that, you can align the rest of it. In fact, whenever I have done that, most things naturally fall into place because the most powerful tool we have is our mind and that can either work against us or for us. The great news is, we are driving and can choose which.

SHARON FULWOOD

Look close to home - what makes your heart sing? Where do you feel useful? I think it is really important to acknowledge your feelings instead of suppressing them. Have some amazing friends who know everything about you and can advocate for you when you need it. Be true to yourself. Respect yourself enough to say no.

STACIE LUSINS

I would suggest doing something that really brings out your joy. When you are in that space, where you feel aligned, trust your instincts and what that voice is telling you. We hold these answers within us; we just need to get to a space where we can trust that and block out the noise and distraction. If you need to bounce ideas, turn to key people in your life. When I do this and I still feel the same excitement after sharing the idea, I'll run with it.

CONTRIBUTOR BIOS

JAYA MCINTYRE
PHOTOGRAPHER

Jaya McIntyre is the driving force behind Empire Art Photography & Coaching and Women Inspired - a professional photographer, coach and creative director with a fierce passion for helping women step into their power. With over 29 years in the creative industry, Jaya combines her deep understanding of storytelling, branding and human behaviour to create transformational experiences, both in front of the lens and behind the scenes.

As a Master NLP and Time Line Therapy practitioner, she brings a unique edge to personal branding and empowerment sessions, blending mindset, visual identity and strategy. Her superpower? Making women feel seen, celebrated and confident in life, and as the face of their brand.

Through her work at Empire Art Photography & Coaching, and the Women Inspired movement, Jaya continues to shine a light on authentic leadership, visibility and what it means to be a woman rewriting her own story

WWW.EMPIREARTPHOTOGRAPHY.COM.AU

MELINDA UYS
EDITOR

Melinda is a versatile writer whose background in education, particularly teaching English and History, has fuelled her passion for crafting witty, meaningful words. Her innate desire to simplify and ease the lives of others has shaped her into the writer she is today.

With a penchant for well-placed and beautiful language, Melinda has become a sought-after content and ghost writer, and editor.

Known for her ability to capture the very essence of scene and emotion, Melinda's talent for painting vivid stories has garnered recognition across Sunshine Coast businesses, the state and internationally.

WWW.MELINDAUYS.COM

ROXANNE MCCARTY–O'KANE
WRITER

Since 2007, Roxanne's unique and multi-award-winning method of storytelling has changed the lives of thousands of budding authors, allowing them to bring their messages to life in nonfiction books with structure, connection to the reader and potential profit.

A prolific ghostwriter, author, workshop facilitator, writing mentor and journalist, Roxanne's presentations are charged with powerful content and tangible tools that remove the mystery from storytelling and ignite a thought-provoking and emotion evoking theatre within the mind.

Her Ignite & Write book series has become a powerful resource for aspiring authors around the world to craft their manuscripts with confidence, clarity and a true sense of purpose and passion. The first book in the trilogy was awarded first place in the 2023 International Reader Views Awards for Best Writing/Publishing Book.

Roxanne has also been recognised as an award-winning businesswoman with the Sunshine Coast Micro/Small Businesswoman of the Year in 2021 and Sunshine Coast Business Awards Creative Industry winner in 2023.

Roxanne's down to earth, humorous style engages her audience and inspires them to think laterally about their own stories and how their lived experiences and knowledge journeys can deeply impact the world around them.

WWW.ROXANNEWRITER.COM

101

A HUGE THANK YOU TO OUR CREATIVE TEAM.

Megan Krolik, Terry McIntyre, @melinadeemakeup, @thehairandmakeupartist_, @rawmakeupandhairstylist

Ladies, it's time to connect!

If you're looking for a dose of inspiration and empowerment, come join us at Women Inspired on social media. Our uplifting community is filled with incredible women who are breaking barriers, pursuing their dreams, and making a positive impact by sharing their story. We believe in the power of sisterhood and supporting each other's journeys. If you or someone you know would like to be a part of our next edition, we welcome you to reach out to us through our website. Together, let's celebrate the remarkable strength and potential within all of us.

WWW.WOMENINSPIRED.COM.AU
WWW.FACEBOOK.COM/WOMENINSPIRED.COM.AU
WWW.INSTAGRAM.COM/WOMENINSPIREDAUSTRALIA

www.ingramcontent.com/pod-product-compliance
Lightning Source LLC
Chambersburg PA
CBHW040317100426
42811CB00012B/1469